Supervised Machine Learning with Python

Develop rich Python coding practices while exploring supervised machine learning

Taylor Smith

BIRMINGHAM - MUMBAI

Supervised Machine Learning with Python

Commissioning Editor: Mrinmayee Kawalkar
Acquisition Editor: Joshua Nadar
Content Development Editor: Ronnel Mathew
Technical Editor: Suwarna Patil
Copy Editor: Safis Editing
Project Coordinator: Hardik Bhinde
Proofreader: Safis Editing
Indexer: Manju Arasan
Graphics: Tom Scaria
Production Coordinator: Shraddha Falebhai

First published: May 2019

Production reference: 1200519

Published by Packt Publishing Ltd.
Livery Place
35 Livery Street
Birmingham
B3 2PB, UK.

ISBN 978-1-83882-566-9

www.packtpub.com

`mapt.io`

Mapt is an online digital library that gives you full access to over 5,000 books and videos, as well as industry leading tools to help you plan your personal development and advance your career. For more information, please visit our website.

Why subscribe?

- Spend less time learning and more time coding with practical eBooks and Videos from over 4,000 industry professionals

- Improve your learning with Skill Plans built especially for you

- Get a free eBook or video every month

- Mapt is fully searchable

- Copy and paste, print, and bookmark content

Packt.com

Did you know that Packt offers eBook versions of every book published, with PDF and ePub files available? You can upgrade to the eBook version at `www.packt.com` and as a print book customer, you are entitled to a discount on the eBook copy. Get in touch with us at `customercare@packtpub.com` for more details.

At `www.packt.com`, you can also read a collection of free technical articles, sign up for a range of free newsletters, and receive exclusive discounts and offers on Packt books and eBooks.

Contributor

About the author

Taylor Smith is a machine learning enthusiast with over five years of experience who loves to apply interesting computational solutions to challenging business problems. Currently working as a principal data scientist, Taylor is also an active open source contributor and staunch Pythonista.

Packt is searching for authors like you

If you're interested in becoming an author for Packt, please visit `authors.packtpub.com` and apply today. We have worked with thousands of developers and tech professionals, just like you, to help them share their insight with the global tech community. You can make a general application, apply for a specific hot topic that we are recruiting an author for, or submit your own idea.

Table of Contents

Preface

Supervised machine learning is used in a wide range of sectors such as finance, online advertising, and analytics because it allows you to train your system to make pricing predictions, campaign adjustments, customer recommendations, and much more, giving the system the ability to self-adjust and make decisions on its own. The benefits this can give make it crucial to know how a machine learns under the hood.

This book will guide you through the implementation and nuances of many popular supervised machine learning algorithms. You'll embark on this journey with a quick overview and see how supervised machine learning differs from unsupervised learning. After that, we will explore parametric models such as linear and logistic regression, non-parametric methods such as decision trees, and various clustering techniques to facilitate decision-making and predictions. As we proceed, you'll work with recommender systems, which are widely used by online companies to increase user interaction and boost potential sales. Finally, we'll wrap up with a brief foray into neural networks and transfer learning.

By the end of this book, you'll be equipped with hands-on techniques to gain the practical know-how needed to quickly and powerfully apply supervised learning algorithms to new problems.

Who this book is for

This book is for aspiring machine learning developers who want to get started with supervised learning. Intermediate knowledge of Python programming and some fundamental knowledge of supervised learning is expected.

What this book covers

Chapter 1, *First Step toward Supervised Learning*, covers the basics of supervised machine learning to get you prepared to start tackling problems on your own. The chapter comprises four important sections. First, we will get our Anaconda environment set up and make sure that we are able to run the examples. Over the next couple of sections following that, we will cover a bit more of the theory behind machine learning, before we start implementing algorithms in the final section, where we'll get our Anaconda environment set up.

Chapter 2, *Implementing Parametric Models*, dives into the guts of several popular supervised learning algorithms within the parametric modeling family. We'll start this section by formally introducing parametric models, then we'll focus on two very popular parametric models in particular: linear and logistic regression. We'll spend some time understanding the inner workings and then jump into Python and actually code them from scratch.

Chapter 3, *Working with Non-Parametric Models*, explores the non-parametric model family. We will start by covering the bias-variance trade-off, and explain how parametric and non-parametric models differ at a fundamental level. We will then get into decision trees and clustering methods. Finally, we'll address some of the pros and cons of non-parametric models.

Chapter 4, *Advanced Topics in Supervised ML*, splits its time between two topics: recommender systems and neural networks. We'll start with collaborative filtering and then talk about integrating content-based similarities into your collaborative filtering systems. Finally, we'll get into neural networks and transfer learning.

To get the most out of this book

You will need the following software to be able to smoothly sail through the chapters:

- Jupyter Notebook
- Anaconda
- Python

Download the example code files

You can download the example code files for this book from your account at www.packt.com. If you purchased this book elsewhere, you can visit www.packt.com/support and register to have the files emailed directly to you.

You can download the code files by following these steps:

1. Log in or register at www.packt.com.
2. Select the **SUPPORT** tab.
3. Click on **Code Downloads & Errata**.
4. Enter the name of the book in the **Search** box and follow the onscreen instructions.

Once the file is downloaded, please make sure that you unzip or extract the folder using the latest version of:

- WinRAR/7-Zip for Windows
- Zipeg/iZip/UnRarX for Mac
- 7-Zip/PeaZip for Linux

The code bundle for the book is also hosted on GitHub at `https://github.com/PacktPublishing/Supervised-Machine-Learning-with-Python`. In case there's an update to the code, it will be updated on the existing GitHub repository.

We also have other code bundles from our rich catalog of books and videos available at `https://github.com/PacktPublishing/`. Check them out!

Download the color images

We also provide a PDF file that has color images of the screenshots/diagrams used in this book. You can download it here: `https://www.packtpub.com/sites/default/files/downloads/9781838825669_ColorImages.pdf`.

Conventions used

There are a number of text conventions used throughout this book.

`CodeInText`: Indicates code words in text, database table names, folder names, filenames, file extensions, pathnames, dummy URLs, user input, and Twitter handles. Here is an example: "Mount the downloaded `WebStorm-10*.dmg` disk image file as another disk in your system."

A block of code is set as follows:

```
from urllib.request import urlretrieve, ProxyHandler, build_opener,
install_opener
import requests
import os
pfx = "https://archive.ics.uci.edu/ml/machine-learning databases/spambase/"
data_dir = "data"
```

Any command-line input or output is written as follows:

```
jupyter notebook
```

Bold: Indicates a new term, an important word, or words that you see onscreen. For example, words in menus or dialog boxes appear in the text like this. Here is an example: "Select **System info** from the **Administration** panel."

 Warnings or important notes appear like this.

 Tips and tricks appear like this.

Get in touch

Feedback from our readers is always welcome.

General feedback: If you have questions about any aspect of this book, mention the book title in the subject of your message and email us at customercare@packtpub.com.

Errata: Although we have taken every care to ensure the accuracy of our content, mistakes do happen. If you have found a mistake in this book, we would be grateful if you would report this to us. Please visit www.packt.com/submit-errata, selecting your book, clicking on the Errata Submission Form link, and entering the details.

Piracy: If you come across any illegal copies of our works in any form on the Internet, we would be grateful if you would provide us with the location address or website name. Please contact us at copyright@packt.com with a link to the material.

If you are interested in becoming an author: If there is a topic that you have expertise in and you are interested in either writing or contributing to a book, please visit authors.packtpub.com.

Reviews

Please leave a review. Once you have read and used this book, why not leave a review on the site that you purchased it from? Potential readers can then see and use your unbiased opinion to make purchase decisions, we at Packt can understand what you think about our products, and our authors can see your feedback on their book. Thank you!

For more information about Packt, please visit packt.com.

1
First Step Towards Supervised Learning

In this book, we will learn about the implementation of many of the common machine learning algorithms you interact with in your daily life. There will be plenty of math, theory, and tangible code examples to satisfy even the biggest machine learning junkie and, hopefully, you'll pick up some useful Python tricks and practices along the way. We are going to start off with a very brief introduction to supervised learning, sharing a real-life machine learning demo; getting our Anaconda environment setup done; learning how to measure the slope of a curve, Nd-curve, and multiple functions; and finally, we'll discuss how we know whether or not a model is good. In this chapter, we will cover the following topics:

- An example of supervised learning in action
- Setting up the environment
- Supervised learning
- Hill climbing and loss functions
- Model evaluation and data splitting

Technical requirements

For this chapter, you will need to install the following software, if you haven't already done so:

- Jupyter Notebook
- Anaconda
- Python

The code files for this chapter can be found at `https://github.com/PacktPublishing/Supervised-Machine-Learning-with-Python`.

An example of supervised learning in action

First, we will take a look at what we can do with supervised machine learning. With the following Terminal prompt, we will launch a new Jupyter Notebook:

```
jupyter notebook
```

Once we are inside this top-level, `Hands-on-Supervised-Machine-Learning-with-Python-master` home directory, we will go directly inside the `examples` directory:

You can see that our only Notebook in here is `1.1 Supervised Learning Demo.ipynb`:

We have the supervised learning demo Jupyter Notebook. We are going to be using a UCI dataset called the `Spam` dataset. This is a list of different emails that contain different features that correspond to spam or not spam. We want to build a machine learning algorithm that can predict whether or not we have an email coming in that is going to be spam. This could be extremely helpful for you if you're running your own email server.

So, the first function in the following code is simply a request's get function. You should already have the dataset, which is already sitting inside the `examples` directory. But in case you don't, you can go ahead and run the following code. You can see that we already have `spam.csv`, so we're not going to download it:

```
from urllib.request import urlretrieve, ProxyHandler, build_opener,
install_opener
import requests
import os
pfx = "https://archive.ics.uci.edu/ml/machine-learning databases/spambase/"
data_dir = "data"
# We might need to set a proxy handler...
try:
    proxies = {"http": os.environ['http_proxy'],
               "https": os.environ['https_proxy']}
    print("Found proxy settings")
    #create the proxy object, assign it to a variable
    proxy = ProxyHandler(proxies)
    # construct a new opener using your proxy settings
    opener = build_opener(proxy)
    # install the opener on the module-level
    install_opener(opener)

except KeyError:
    pass
# The following will download the data if you don't already have it...
def get_data(link, where):
    # Append the prefix
    link = pfx + link
```

Next, we will use the `pandas` library. This is a data analysis library from Python. You can install it when we go through the next stage, which is the environment setup. This library is a data frame data structure that is a kind of native Python, which we will use as follows:

```
import pandas as pd
names = ["word_freq_make", "word_freq_address", "word_freq_all",
         "word_freq_3d", "word_freq_our", "word_freq_over",
         "word_freq_remove", "word_freq_internet", "word_freq_order",
         "word_freq_mail", "word_freq_receive", "word_freq_will",
         "word_freq_people", "word_freq_report", "word_freq_addresses",
         "word_freq_free", "word_freq_business", "word_freq_email",
         "word_freq_you", "word_freq_credit", "word_freq_your",
         "word_freq_font", "word_freq_000", "word_freq_money",
         "word_freq_hp", "word_freq_hpl", "word_freq_george",
         "word_freq_650", "word_freq_lab", "word_freq_labs",
         "word_freq_telnet", "word_freq_857", "word_freq_data",
         "word_freq_415", "word_freq_85", "word_freq_technology",
```

```
           "word_freq_1999", "word_freq_parts", "word_freq_pm",
           "word_freq_direct", "word_freq_cs", "word_freq_meeting",
           "word_freq_original", "word_freq_project", "word_freq_re",
           "word_freq_edu", "word_freq_table", "word_freq_conference",
           "char_freq_;", "char_freq_(", "char_freq_[", "char_freq_!",
           "char_freq_$", "char_freq_#", "capital_run_length_average",
           "capital_run_length_longest", "capital_run_length_total",
           "is_spam"]
df = pd.read_csv(os.path.join("data", "spam.csv"), header=None,
names=names)
# pop off the target
y = df.pop("is_spam")
df.head()
```

This allows us to lay out our data in the following format. We can use all sorts of different statistical functions that are nice to use when you're doing machine learning:

Out[2]:		word_freq_make	word_freq_address	word_freq_all	word_freq_3d	word_freq_our	word_freq_over	word_freq_remove	word_freq_internet
	0	0.00	0.64	0.64	0.0	0.32	0.00	0.00	0.00
	1	0.21	0.28	0.50	0.0	0.14	0.28	0.21	0.07
	2	0.06	0.00	0.71	0.0	1.23	0.19	0.19	0.12
	3	0.00	0.00	0.00	0.0	0.63	0.00	0.31	0.63
	4	0.00	0.00	0.00	0.0	0.63	0.00	0.31	0.63
	5 rows × 57 columns								

If some of this terminology is not familiar to you, don't panic yet—we will learn about these terminologies in detail over the course of the book.

For train_test_split, we will take the df dataset and split it into two parts: train set and test set. In addition to that, we have the target, which is a 01 variable that indicates true or false for spam or not spam. We will split that as well, which includes the corresponding vector of true or false labels. By splitting the labels, we get 3680 training samples and 921 test samples, file as shown in the following code snippet:

```
from sklearn.model_selection import train_test_split
X_train, X_test, y_train, y_test = train_test_split(df, y, test_size=0.2,
random_state=42, stratify=y)
print("Num training samples: %i" % X_train.shape[0])
print("Num test samples: %i" % X_test.shape[0])
```

The output of the preceding code is as follows:

```
Num training samples: 3680
Num test samples: 921
```

 Notice that we have a lot more training samples than test samples, which is important for fitting our models. We will learn about this later in the book. So, don't worry too much about what's going on here, as this is all just for demo purposes.

In the following code, we have the `packtml` library. This is the actual package that we are building, which is a classification and regression tree classifier. `CARTClassifier` is simply a generalization of a decision tree for both regression and classification purposes. Everything we fit here is going to be a supervised machine learning algorithm that we build from scratch. This is one of the classifiers that we are going to build in this book. We also have this utility function for plotting a learning curve. This is going to take our train set and break it into different folds for cross-validation. We will fit the training set in different stages of numbers of training samples, so we can see how the learning curve converges between the train and validation folds, which determines how our algorithm is learning, essentially:

```
from packtml.utils.plotting import plot_learning_curve
from packtml.decision_tree import CARTClassifier
from sklearn.metrics import accuracy_score
import numpy as np
import matplotlib.pyplot as plt
%matplotlib inline
# very basic decision tree
plot_learning_curve(
        CARTClassifier, metric=accuracy_score,
        X=X_train, y=y_train, n_folds=3, seed=21, trace=True,
        train_sizes=(np.linspace(.25, .75, 4) *
X_train.shape[0]).astype(int),
        max_depth=8, random_state=42)\
    .show()
```

We will go ahead and run the preceding code and plot how the algorithm has learned across the different sizes of our training set. You can see we're going to fit it for 4 different training set sizes at 3 folds of cross-validation.

So, what we're actually doing is fitting 12 separate models, which will take a few seconds to run:

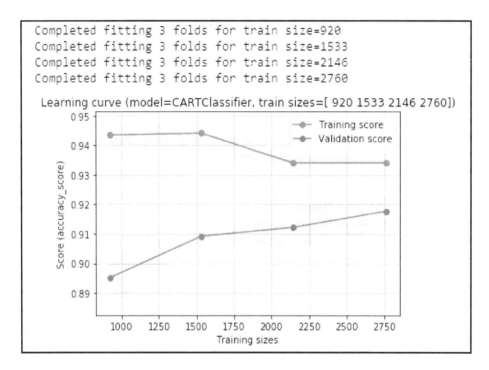

```
Completed fitting 3 folds for train size=920
Completed fitting 3 folds for train size=1533
Completed fitting 3 folds for train size=2146
Completed fitting 3 folds for train size=2760
```

In the preceding output, we can see our **Training score** and our **Validation score**. The **Training score** diminishes as it learns to generalize, and our **Validation score** increases as it learns to generalize from the training set to the validation set. So, our accuracy is hovering right around 92-93% on our validation set.

We will use the hyperparameters from the very best one here:

```
decision_tree = CARTClassifier(X_train, y_train, random_state=42,
max_depth=8)
```

Logistic regression

In this section, we will learn about logistic regression, which is another classification model that we're going to build from scratch. We will go ahead and fit the following code:

```
from packtml.regression import SimpleLogisticRegression
# simple logistic regression classifier
plot_learning_curve(
```

```
        SimpleLogisticRegression, metric=accuracy_score,
        X=X_train, y=y_train, n_folds=3, seed=21, trace=True,
        train_sizes=(np.linspace(.25, .8, 4) *
X_train.shape[0]).astype(int),
        n_steps=250, learning_rate=0.0025, loglik_interval=100)\
    .show()
```

This is much faster than the decision tree. In the following output, you can see that we converge a lot more around the 92.5% range. This looks a little more consistent than our decision tree, but it doesn't perform quite well enough on the validation set:

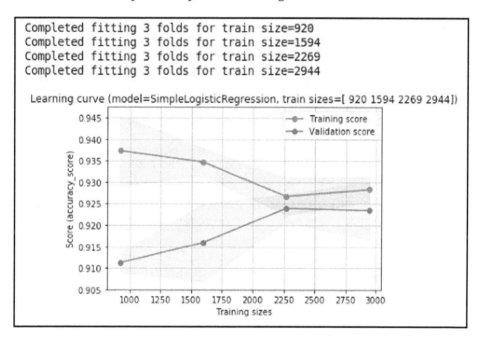

In the following screenshot, there are encoded records of spam emails. We will see how this encoding performs on an email that we can read and validate. So, if you have visited the UCI link that was included at the top of the Jupyter Notebook, it will provide a description of all the features inside the dataset. We have a lot of different features here that are counting the ratio of particular words to the number of words in the entire email. Some of those words might be free and some credited. We also have a couple of other features that are counting character frequencies, the number of exclamation points, and the number of concurrent capital runs.

So, if you have a really highly capitalized set of words, we have all these features:

```
| SPAM E-MAIL DATABASE ATTRIBUTES (in .names format)
|
| 48 continuous real [0,100] attributes of type word_freq_WORD
| = percentage of words in the e-mail that match WORD,
| i.e. 100 * (number of times the WORD appears in the e-mail) /
| total number of words in e-mail.  A "word" in this case is any
| string of alphanumeric characters bounded by non-alphanumeric
| characters or end-of-string.
|
| 6 continuous real [0,100] attributes of type char_freq_CHAR
| = percentage of characters in the e-mail that match CHAR,
| i.e. 100 * (number of CHAR occurences) / total characters in e-mail
|
| 1 continuous real [1,...] attribute of type capital_run_length_average
| = average length of uninterrupted sequences of capital letters
|
| 1 continuous integer [1,...] attribute of type capital_run_length_longest
| = length of longest uninterrupted sequence of capital letters
|
| 1 continuous integer [1,...] attribute of type capital_run_length_total
| = sum of length of uninterrupted sequences of capital letters
| = total number of capital letters in the e-mail
|
| 1 nominal {0,1} class attribute of type spam
| = denotes whether the e-mail was considered spam (1) or not (0),
```

In the following screenshot, we will create two emails. The first email is very obviously spam. Even if anyone gets this email, no one will respond to it:

```
spam_email = """
Dear small business owner,
This email is to inform you that for $0 down, you can receive a
FREE CREDIT REPORT!!! Your money is important; PROTECT YOUR CREDIT and
reply direct to us for assistance!
"""

print(spam_email)
```

The output of the preceding code snippet is as follows:

```
Dear small business owner,
This email is to inform you that for $0 down, you can receive a
FREE CREDIT REPORT!!! Your money is important; PROTECT YOUR CREDIT and
reply direct to us for assistance!
```

The second email looks less like spam:

```
Hey George,

Make sure to be careful when checking your HP email. There has been a
phishing attempt recently advertising a credit report. This is a known scam,
and should be ignored. Please feel free to let me know if you have any
questions or concerns, but the IT guys told me to warn everyone.
```

The model that we have just fit is going to look at both of the emails and encode the features, and will classify which is, and which is not, spam.

The following function is going to encode those emails into the features we discussed. Initially, we're going to use a `Counter` function as an object, and tokenize our emails. All we're doing is splitting our email into a list of words, and then the words can be split into a list of characters. Later, we'll count the characters and words so that we can generate our features:

```python
from collections import Counter
import numpy as np
def encode_email(email):
    # tokenize the email
    tokens = email.split()
    # easiest way to count characters will be to join everything
    # up and split them into chars, then use a counter to count them
    # all ONE time.
    chars = list("".join(tokens))
    char_counts = Counter(chars)
    n_chars = len(chars)
    # we can do the same thing with "tokens" to get counts of words
    # (but we want them to be lowercase!)
    word_counts = Counter([t.lower() for t in tokens])
    # Of the names above, the ones that start with "word" are
    # percentages of frequencies of words. Let's get the words
    # in question
    freq_words = [
        name.split("_")[-1]
        for name in names
        if name.startswith("word")
    ]
    # compile the first 48 values using the words in question
    word_freq_encodings = [100. * (word_counts.get(t, 0) / len(tokens))
                           for t in freq_words]
```

So, all those features that we have up at the beginning tell us what words we're interested in counting. We can see that the original dataset is interested in counting words such as address, email, business, and credit, and then, for our characters, we're looking for opened and closed parentheses and dollar signs (which are quite relevant to our spam emails). So, we're going to count all of those shown as follows:

```
In [2]: import pandas as pd

        names = ["word_freq_make", "word_freq_address", "word_freq_all",
                 "word_freq_3d", "word_freq_our", "word_freq_over",
                 "word_freq_remove", "word_freq_internet", "word_freq_order",
                 "word_freq_mail", "word_freq_receive", "word_freq_will",
                 "word_freq_people", "word_freq_report", "word_freq_addresses",
                 "word_freq_free", "word_freq_business", "word_freq_email",
                 "word_freq_you", "word_freq_credit", "word_freq_your",
                 "word_freq_font", "word_freq_000", "word_freq_money",
                 "word_freq_hp", "word_freq_hpl", "word_freq_george",
                 "word_freq_650", "word_freq_lab", "word_freq_labs",
                 "word_freq_telnet", "word_freq_857", "word_freq_data",
                 "word_freq_415", "word_freq_85", "word_freq_technology",
                 "word_freq_1999", "word_freq_parts", "word_freq_pm",
                 "word_freq_direct", "word_freq_cs", "word_freq_meeting",
                 "word_freq_original", "word_freq_project", "word_freq_re",
                 "word_freq_edu", "word_freq_table", "word_freq_conference",
                 "char_freq_;", "char_freq_(", "char_freq_[", "char_freq_!",
                 "char_freq_$", "char_freq_#", "capital_run_length_average",
                 "capital_run_length_longest", "capital_run_length_total",
                 "is_spam"]

        df = pd.read_csv(os.path.join("data", "spam.csv"), header=None, names=names)

        # pop off the target
        y = df.pop("is_spam")
        df.head()
```

Apply the ratio and keep track of the total number of `capital_runs`, computing the mean average, maximum, and minimum:

```
# make a np array to compute the next few stats quickly
capital_runs = np.asarray(capital_runs)
    capital_stats = [capital_runs.mean(),
                     capital_runs.max(),
                     capital_runs.sum()]
```

When we run the preceding code, we get the following output. This is going to encode our emails. This is just simply a vector of all the different features. It should be about 50 characters long:

```
# get the email vectors
fake_email = encode_email(spam_email)
real_email = encode_email(not_spam)
# this is what they look like:
```

```
print("Spam email:")
print(fake_email)
print("\nReal email:")
print(real_email)
```

The output of the preceding code is as follows:

```
Spam email:
[  0.           0.           0.           0.           0.           0.           0.
   0.           0.           0.           2.85714286   0.           0.           0.
   0.           2.85714286   2.85714286   2.85714286   5.71428571
   5.71428571   5.71428571   0.           0.           2.85714286   0.           0.
   0.           0.           0.           0.           0.           0.           0.
   0.           0.           0.           0.           0.           0.
   2.85714286   0.           0.           0.           0.           0.           0.
   0.           0.           0.61728395   0.           0.           2.4691358
   0.61728395   0.           7.2          17.          36.        ]

Real email:
[  1.81818182   0.           0.           0.           0.           0.           0.
   0.           0.           0.           0.           0.           0.           0.
   0.           1.81818182   0.           0.           1.81818182
   1.81818182   1.81818182   0.           0.           0.           1.81818182
   0.           0.           0.           0.           0.           0.           0.
   0.           0.           0.           0.           0.           0.           0.
   0.           0.           0.           0.           0.           0.           0.
   0.           1.25         2.          10.        ]
```

When we fit the preceding values into our models, we will see whether our model is any good. So, ideally, we will see that the actual fake email is predicted to be fake, and the actual real email is predicted to be real. So, if the emails are predicted as fake, our spam prediction is indeed spam for both the decision tree and the logistic regression. Our true email is not spam, which perhaps is even more important, because we don't want to filter real email into the spam folder. So, you can see that we fitted some pretty good models here that apply to something that we would visually inspect as true spam or not:

```
predict = (lambda rec, mod: "SPAM!" if mod.predict([rec])[0] == 1 else "Not
spam")

print("Decision tree predictions:")
print("Spam email prediction: %r" % predict(fake_email, decision_tree))
print("Real email prediction: %r" % predict(real_email, decision_tree))

print("\nLogistic regression predictions:")
print("Spam email prediction: %r" % predict(fake_email,
logistic_regression))
print("Real email prediction: %r" % predict(real_email,
logistic_regression))
```

The output of the preceding code is as follows:

```
Decision tree predictions:
Spam email prediction: 'SPAM!'
Real email prediction: 'Not spam'

Logistic regression predictions:
Spam email prediction: 'SPAM!'
Real email prediction: 'Not spam'
```

This is a demo of the actual algorithms that we're going to build from scratch in this book, and can be applied to real-world problems.

Setting up the environment

We will go ahead and get our environment set up. Now that we have walked through the preceding example, let's go ahead and get our Anaconda environment set up. Among other things, Anaconda is a dependency management tool that will allow us to control specific versioning of each of the packages that we want to use. We will go to the Anaconda website through this link, `https://www.anaconda.com/download/`, and click on the **Download** tab.

 The package that we're building is not going to work with Python 2.7. So, once you have Anaconda, we will perform a live coding example of an actual package setup, as well as the environment setup that's included in the `.yml` file that we built.

Once you have Anaconda set up inside the home directory, we are going to use the `environment.yml` file. You can see that the name of the environment we're going to create is `packt-sml` for supervised machine learning. We will need NumPy, SciPy, scikit-learn, and pandas. These are all scientific computing and data analysis libraries. Matplotlib is what we were using to plot those plots inside the Jupyter Notebook, so you're going to need all those plots. The `conda` package makes it really easy to build this environment. All we have to do is type `conda env create` and then `-f` to point it to the file, go to `Hands-on-Supervised-Machine-Learning-with-Python-master`, and we're going to use the `environment.yml` as shown in the following command:

```
cat environment.yml
conda env create -f environment.yml
```

As this is the first time you're creating this, it will create a large script that will download everything you need. Once you have created your environment, you need to activate it. So, on a macOS or a Linux machine, we will type `source activate packt-sml`.

If you're on Windows, simply type `activate packt-sml`, which will activate that environment:

```
source activate packt-sml
```

The output is as follows:

```
test@test-Veriton-Series:~/Downloads/Hands-on-Supervised-Machine-Learning-with-Python-master$ conda env create -f environment.yml

CondaValueError: prefix already exists: /home/test/anaconda3/envs/packt-sml

test@test-Veriton-Series:~/Downloads/Hands-on-Supervised-Machine-Learning-with-Python-master$ source activate packt-sml
(packt-sml) test@test-Veriton-Series:~/Downloads/Hands-on-Supervised-Machine-Learning-with-Python-master$
```

In order to build the package, we will type the `cat setup.py` command. We can inspect this quickly:

```
cat setup.py
```

Take a look at this `setup.py`. Basically, this is just using setup tools to install the package. In the following screenshot, we see all the different sub models:

```
(packt-sml) test@test-Veriton-Series:~/Documents/Hands-on-Supervised-Machine-Learning-with-Python-master$ cat setup.py
# -*- coding: utf-8 -*-

from __future__ import absolute_import

import sys
import setuptools

with open("packtml/VERSION", 'r') as vsn:
    VERSION = vsn.read().strip()

# Permitted args: "install" only, basically.
UNSUPPORTED_COMMANDS = {  # this is a set literal, not a dict
    'develop', 'release', 'bdist_egg', 'bdist_rpm',
    'bdist_wininst', 'install_egg_info', 'build_sphinx',
    'egg_info', 'easy_install', 'upload', 'bdist_wheel',
    '--single-version-externally-managed', 'test', 'build_ext'
}

intersect = UNSUPPORTED_COMMANDS.intersection(set(sys.argv))
if intersect:
    msg = "The following arguments are unsupported: %s. " \
          "To install, please use 'python setup.py install'." \
          % str(list(intersect))

    # if "test" is in the arguments, make sure the user knows how to test.
    if "test" in intersect:
        msg += " To test, make sure pytest is installed, and after " \
               "installation run 'pytest packtml'"

    raise ValueError(msg)

# get requirements
with open("requirements.txt") as req:
    REQUIREMENTS = req.read().strip().split("\n")

py_version_tag = '-%s.%s'.format(sys.version_info[:2])
setuptools.setup(name="packtml",
                 description="Hands-on Supervised Learning · teach a machine "
                             "to think for itself!",
                 author="Taylor G Smith",
                 author_email="taylor.smith@alkaline-ml.com",
                 packages=['packtml',
                           'packtml/clustering',
                           'packtml/decision_tree',
                           'packtml/metrics',
                           'packtml/neural_net',
                           'packtml/recommendation',
                           'packtml/regression',
                           'packtml/utils'],
                 zip_safe=False,
                 include_package_data=True,
```

We will build the package by typing the `python setup.py install` command. Now, when we go into Python and try to import `packtml`, we get the following output:

```
(packt-sml) test@test-Veriton-Series:~/Desktop/Code/Hands-on-Supervised-Machine-Learning-with-Python-master$ python setup.py install
running install
running bdist_egg
running egg_info
creating packtml.egg-info
writing packtml.egg-info/PKG-INFO
writing dependency_links to packtml.egg-info/dependency_links.txt
writing requirements to packtml.egg-info/requires.txt
writing top-level names to packtml.egg-info/top_level.txt
writing manifest file 'packtml.egg-info/SOURCES.txt'
reading manifest file 'packtml.egg-info/SOURCES.txt'
reading manifest template 'MANIFEST.in'
warning: manifest_maker: MANIFEST.in, line 1: unknown action 'recursive'

writing manifest file 'packtml.egg-info/SOURCES.txt'
installing library code to build/bdist.linux-x86_64/egg
running install_lib
running build_py
creating build
creating build/lib
creating build/lib/packtml
copying packtml/__init__.py -> build/lib/packtml
copying packtml/base.py -> build/lib/packtml
creating build/lib/packtml/clustering
copying packtml/clustering/knn.py -> build/lib/packtml/clustering
copying packtml/clustering/__init__.py -> build/lib/packtml/clustering
creating build/lib/packtml/decision_tree
copying packtml/decision_tree/cart.py -> build/lib/packtml/decision_tree
copying packtml/decision_tree/__init__.py -> build/lib/packtml/decision_tree
copying packtml/decision_tree/metrics.py -> build/lib/packtml/decision_tree
creating build/lib/packtml/metrics
copying packtml/metrics/__init__.py -> build/lib/packtml/metrics
copying packtml/metrics/ranking.py -> build/lib/packtml/metrics
creating build/lib/packtml/neural_net
copying packtml/neural_net/__init__.py -> build/lib/packtml/neural_net
copying packtml/neural_net/base.py -> build/lib/packtml/neural_net
copying packtml/neural_net/transfer.py -> build/lib/packtml/neural_net
copying packtml/neural_net/mlp.py -> build/lib/packtml/neural_net
creating build/lib/packtml/recommendation
copying packtml/recommendation/__init__.py -> build/lib/packtml/recommendation
copying packtml/recommendation/base.py -> build/lib/packtml/recommendation
copying packtml/recommendation/als.py -> build/lib/packtml/recommendation
copying packtml/recommendation/itemitem.py -> build/lib/packtml/recommendation
copying packtml/recommendation/data.py -> build/lib/packtml/recommendation
creating build/lib/packtml/regression
copying packtml/regression/__init__.py -> build/lib/packtml/regression
copying packtml/regression/simple_logistic.py -> build/lib/packtml/regression
copying packtml/regression/simple_regression.py -> build/lib/packtml/regression
creating build/lib/packtml/utils
copying packtml/utils/linalg.py -> build/lib/packtml/utils
copying packtml/utils/extmath.py -> build/lib/packtml/utils
copying packtml/utils/__init__.py -> build/lib/packtml/utils
copying packtml/utils/validation.py -> build/lib/packtml/utils
copying packtml/utils/plotting.py -> build/lib/packtml/utils
copying packtml/VERSION -> build/lib/packtml
creating build/bdist.linux-x86_64
creating build/bdist.linux-x86_64/egg
```

In this section, we have installed the environment and built the package. In the next section, we will start covering some of the theory behind supervised machine learning.

Supervised learning

In this section, we will formally define what machine learning is and, specifically, what supervised machine learning is.

In the early days of AI, everything was a rules engine. The programmer wrote the function and the rules, and the computer simply followed them. Modern-day AI is more in line with machine learning, which teaches a computer to write its own functions. Some may contest that oversimplification of the concept, but, at its core, this is largely what machine learning is all about.

We're going to look at a quick example of what machine learning is and what it is not. Here, we're using scikit-learn's datasets, submodule to create two objects and variables, also known as covariance or features, which are along the column axis. y is a vector with the same number of values as there are rows in X. In this case, y is a class label. For the sake of an example, y here could be a binary label corresponding to a real-world occurrence, such as the malignancy of a tumor. X is then a matrix of attributes that describe y. One feature could be the diameter of the tumor, and another could indicate its density. The preceding explanation can be seen in the following code:

```
import numpy as np
from sklearn.datasets import make_classification

rs = np.random.RandomState(42)
X,y = make_classification(n_samples=10, random_state=rs)
```

A rules engine, by our definition, is simply business logic. It can be as simple or as complex as you need it to be, but the programmer makes the rules. In this function, we're going to evaluate our X matrix by returning 1, or `true`, where the sums over the rows are greater than 0. Even though there's some math involved here, there is still a rules engine, because we, the programmers, defined a rule. So, we could theoretically get into a gray area, where the rule itself was discovered via machine learning. But, for the sake of argument, let's take an example that the head surgeon arbitrarily picks 0 as our threshold, and anything above that is deemed as cancerous:

```
def make_life_alterning_decision(X):
    """Determine whether something big happens"""
    row_sums = X.sum(axis=1)
    return (row_sums > 0).astype(int)
make_life_alterning_decision(X)
```

The output of the preceding code snippet is as follows:

```
array([0, 1, 0, 0, 1, 1, 1, 0, 1, 0])
```

Now, as mentioned before, our rules engine can be as simple or as complex as we want it to be. Here, we're not only interested in `row_sums`, but we have several criteria to meet in order to deem something cancerous. The minimum value in the row must be less than -1.5, in addition to one or more of the following three criteria:

- The row sum exceeds 0
- The sum of the rows is evenly divisible by 0.5
- The maximum value of the row is greater than 1.5

So, even though our math is a little more complex here, we're still just building a rules engine:

```python
def make_more_complex_life_alterning_decision(X):
    """Make a more complicated decision about something big"""
    row_sums = X.sum(axis=1)
      return ((X.min(axis=1) < -1.5) &
                ((row_sums >= 0.) |
                (row_sums % 0.5 == 0) |
                (X.max(axis=1) > 1.5))).astype(int)

make_more_complex_life_alterning_decision(X)
```

The output of the preceding code is as follows:

```
array([0, 1, 1, 1, 1, 1, 0, 1, 1, 0])
```

Now, let's say that our surgeon understands and realizes they're not the math or programming whiz that they thought they were. So, they hire programmers to build them a machine learning model. The model itself is a function that discovers parameters that complement a decision function, which is essentially the function the machine itself learned. So, parameters are things we'll discuss in our next Chapter 2, *Implementing Parametric Models,* which are parametric models. So, what's happening behind the scenes when we invoke the `fit` method is that the model learns the characteristics and patterns of the data, and how the X matrix describes the y vector. Then, when we call the `predict` function, it applies its learned decision function to the input data to make an educated guess:

```python
from sklearn.linear_model import LogisticRegression

def learn_life_lession(X, y):
    """Learn a lesson abd apply it in a future situation"""
    model = LogisticRegression().fit(X, y)
    return (lambda X: model.predict(X))
educated_decision = learn_life_lession(X, y)(X)
educated_decision
```

The output of the preceding code is as follows:

```
array([1, 1, 0, 0, 0, 1, 1, 0, 1, 0])
```

So, now we're at a point where we need to define specifically what supervised learning is. Supervised learning is precisely the example we just described previously. Given our matrix of examples, X, in a vector of corresponding labels, y, that learns a function which approximates the value of y or $\hat{y}$:

$$\hat{y} = f(X, y; \theta)$$

There are other forms of machine learning that are not supervised, known as **unsupervised machine learning**. These do not have labels and are more geared toward pattern recognition tasks. So, what makes something supervised is the presence of labeled data.

Going back to our previous example, when we invoke the `fit` method, we learn our new decision function and then, when we call `predict`, we're approximating the new y values. So, the output is this $\hat{y}$ we just looked at:

ML: a simple example

```
from sklearn.linear_model import LogisticRegression

def learn_life_lesson(X, y):
    """Learn a lesson and apply it in a future situation"""
    model = LogisticRegression().fit(X, y)
    return (lambda x: model.predict(x))

# learn a lesson and THEN make a decision
educated_decision = learn_life_lesson(X, y)(X)
educated_decision

array([1, 1, 0, 0, 0, 1, 1, 0, 1, 0])
```

Learn our function *f*

Apply *f* to the data to produce predictions

Supervised learning learns a function from labelled samples that approximates future y values. At this point, you should feel comfortable explaining the abstract concept—just the high-level idea of what supervised machine learning is.

Hill climbing and loss functions

In the last section, we got comfortable with the idea of supervised machine learning. Now, we will learn how exactly a machine learns underneath the hood. This section is going to examine a common optimization technique used by many machine learning algorithms, called **hill climbing**. It is predicated on the fact that each problem has an ideal state and a way to measure how close or how far we are from that. It is important to note that not all machine learning algorithms use this approach.

Loss functions

First, we'll cover loss functions, and then, prior to diving into hill climbing and descent, we'll take a quick math refresher.

 There's going to be some math in this lesson, and while we try to shy away from the purely theoretical concepts, this is something that we simply have to get through in order to understand the guts of most of these algorithms. There will be a brief applied section at the end. Don't panic if you can't remember some of the calculus; just simply try to grasp what is happening behind the black box.

So, as mentioned before, a machine learning algorithm has to measure how close it is to some objective. We define this as a cost function, or a loss function. Sometimes, we hear it referred to as an objective function. Although not all machine learning algorithms are designed to directly minimize a loss function, we're going to learn the rule here rather than the exception. The point of a loss function is to determine the goodness of a model fit. It is typically evaluated over the course of a model's learning procedure and converges when the model has maximized its learning capacity.

A typical loss function computes a scalar value which is given by the true labels and the predicted labels. That is, given our actual y and our predicted y, which is $\hat{y}$. This notation might be cryptic, but all it means is that some function, L, which we're going to call our loss function, is going to accept the ground truth, which is y and the predictions, $\hat{y}$, and return some scalar value. The typical formula for the loss function is given as follows:

$$\mathcal{L}(y, \hat{y})E \in \mathbb{R}$$

So, I've listed several common loss functions here, which may or may not look familiar. **Sum of Squared Error (SSE)** is a metric that we're going to be using for our regression models:

$$SumofSquaredError(SSE) = \sum_{i=1}^{n}(y_i - \hat{y}_i)^2$$

Cross entropy is a very commonly used classification metric:

$$BinaryCrossEntropy = -\sum_{x}p(x)log(1 - p(x))$$

In the following diagram, the L function on the left is simply indicating that it is our loss function over y and $\hat{y}$ given parameter theta. So, for any algorithm, we want to find the set of the theta parameters that minimize the loss. That is, if we're predicting the cost of a house, for example, we may want to estimate the cost per square foot as accurately as possible so as to minimize how wrong we are.

Parameters are often in a much higher dimensional space than can be represented visually. So, the big question we're concerned with is the following: How can we minimize the cost? It is typically not feasible for us to attempt every possible value to determine the true minimum of a problem. So, we have to find a way to descend this nebulous hill of loss. The tough part is that, at any given point, we don't know whether the curve goes up or down without some kind of evaluation. And that's precisely what we want to avoid, because it's very expensive:

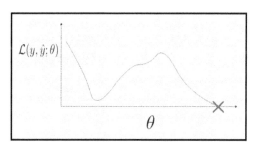

We can describe this problem as waking up in a pitch-black room with an uneven floor and trying to find the lowest point in the room. You don't know how big the room is. You don't know how deep or how high it gets. Where do you step first? One thing we can do is to examine exactly where we stand and determine which direction around us slopes downward. To do that, we have to measure the slope of the curve.

Measuring the slope of a curve

The following is a quick refresher on scalar derivatives. To compute the slope at any given point, the standard way is to typically measure the slope of the line between the point we're interested in and some secant point, which we'll call delta x:

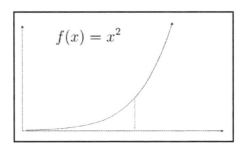

As the distance between x and its neighbor delta x approaches 0, or as our limit approaches 0, we arrive at the slope of the curve. This is given by the following formula:

$$\frac{d}{dx} = f'(x) = \lim_{\triangle x \to 0} = \frac{f(x + \triangle x) - f(x)}{\triangle x}$$

There are several different notations that you may be familiar with. One is f prime of x. The slope of a constant is 0. So, if $f(x)$ is 9, in other words, if y is simply 9, it never changes. There is no slope. So, the slope is 0, as shown:

$$\frac{d}{dx} 9 = 0$$

We can also see the power law in effect here in the second example. This will come in useful later on. If we multiply the variable by the power, and decrement the power by one, we get the following:

$$\frac{d}{dx} 3x^2 = 6x$$

Measuring the slope of an Nd-curve

In order to measure the slope of a vector or a multi-dimensional surface, we will introduce the idea of partial derivatives, which are simply derivatives with respect to a variable, with all the other variables held as constants. So, our solution is a vector of dimension k, where k is the number of variables that our function takes. In this case, we have x and y. Each respective position in the vector that we solve is a derivative with respect to the corresponding function's positional variable.

From a conceptual level, what we're doing is we're holding one of the variables still and changing the other variables around it to see how the slope changes. Our denominator's notation indicates which variable we're measuring the slope with, with respect to that point. So, in this case, the first position, $d(x)$, is showing that we're taking the partial derivative of function f with respect to x, where we hold y constant. And then, likewise, in the second one, we're taking the derivative of function f with respect to y, holding x constant. So, what we get in the end is called a gradient, which is a super keyword. It is simply just a vector of partial derivatives:

$$f(x, y) = 4x^3 y$$

$$\nabla f(x, y) = [\frac{\partial f(x, y)}{\partial x}, \frac{\partial f(x, y)}{\partial y}] = [12x^2 y, 4x^3]$$

Measuring the slope of multiple functions

We want to get really complicated, though, and measure the slopes of multiple functions at the same time. All we'll end up with is a matrix of gradients along the rows. In the following formula, we can see the solution that we just solved from the previous example:

$$f(x, y) = 4x^3 y$$

In the next formula, we have introduced this new function, called g. We see the gradient for function g, with each position corresponding to the partial derivative with respect to the variables x and y:

$$g(x, y) = 2x + y^3$$

When we stack these together into a matrix, what we get is a Jacobian. You don't need to solve this, but you should understand that what we're doing is taking the slope of a multi-dimensional surface. You can treat it as a bit of a black box as long as you understand that. This is exactly how we're computing the gradient and the Jacobian:

$$\begin{bmatrix} \nabla f(x,y) \\ \nabla g(x,y) \end{bmatrix} = \begin{bmatrix} \frac{\partial f(x,y)}{\partial x} & \frac{\partial f(x,y)}{\partial y} \\ \frac{\partial g(x,y)}{\partial x} & \frac{\partial g(x,y)}{\partial y} \end{bmatrix} = \begin{bmatrix} 12x^2 y & 4x^3 \\ 2 & 3y^2 \end{bmatrix}$$

Hill climbing and descent

We will go back to our example—the lost hill that we looked at. We want to find a way to select a set of theta parameters that is going to minimize our loss function, *L*. As we've already established, we need to climb or descend the hill, and understand where we are with respect to our neighboring points without having to compute everything. To do that, we need to be able to measure the slope of the curve with respect to the theta parameters. So, going back to our house example, as mentioned before, we want to know how much correct the incremental value of cost per square foot makes. Once we know that, we can start taking directional steps toward finding the best estimate. So, if you make a bad guess, you can turn around and go in exactly the other direction. So, we can either climb or descend the hill depending on our metric, which allows us to optimize the parameters of a function that we want to learn irrespective of how the function itself performs. This is a layer of abstraction. This optimization process is called gradient descent, and it supports many of the machine learning algorithms that we will discuss in this book.

The following code shows a simple example of how we can measure the gradient of a matrix with respect to theta. This example is actually a simplified snippet of the learning component of logistic regression:

```
import numpy as np

seed = (42)

X = np.random.RandomState(seed).rand(5, 3).round(4)

y = np.array([1, 1, 0, 1, 0])

h = (lambda X: 1. / (1. + np.exp(-X)))

theta = np.zeros(3)

lam = 0.05
```

```
def iteration(theta):

    y_hat = h(X.dot(theta))

    residuals = y - y_hat

    gradient = X.T.dot(residuals)
    theta += gradient * lam
    print("y hat: %r" % y_hat.round(3).tolist())
    print("Gradient: %r" % gradient.round(3).tolist())
    print("New theta: %r\n" % theta.round(3).tolist())

iteration(theta)
iteration(theta)
```

At the very top, we randomly initialize X and y, which is not part of the algorithm. So, x here is the sigmoid function, also called the **logistic function**. The word logistic comes from logistic progression. This is a necessary transformation that is applied in logistic regression. Just understand that we have to apply that; it's part of the function. So, we initialize our theta vector, with respect to which we're going to compute our gradient as zeros. Again, all of them are zeros. Those are our parameters. Now, for each iteration, we're going to get our $\hat{y}$, which is our estimated y, if you recall. We get that by taking the dot product of our X matrix against our theta parameters, pushed through that logistic function, h, which is our $\hat{y}$.

Now, we want to compute the gradient of that dot product between the residuals and the input matrix, X, of our predictors. The way we compute our residuals is simply y minus $\hat{y}$, which gives the residuals. Now, we have our $\hat{y}$. How do we get the gradient? The gradient is just the dot product between the input matrix, X, and those residuals. We will use that gradient to determine which direction we need to step in. The way we do that is we add the gradient to our theta vector. Lambda regulates how quickly we step up or down that gradient. So, it's our learning rate. If you think of it as a step size—going back to that dark room example—if it's too large, it's easy to overstep the lowest point. But if it's too small, you're going to spend forever inching around the room. So, it's a bit of a balancing act, but it allows us to regulate the pace at which we update our theta values and descend our gradient. Again, this algorithm is something we will cover in the next chapter.

We get the output of the preceding code as follows:

```
y hat: [0.5, 0.5, 0.5, 0.5, 0.5]
Gradient: [0.395, 0.024, 0.538]
New theta: [0.02, 0.001, 0.027]

y hat: [0.507, 0.504, 0.505, 0.51, 0.505]
Gradient: [0.378, 0.012, 0.518]
New theta: [0.039, 0.002, 0.053]
```

This example demonstrates how our gradient or slope actually changes as we adjust our coefficients and vice versa.

In the next section, we will see how to evaluate our models and learn the cryptic `train_test_split`.

Model evaluation and data splitting

In this chapter, we will define what it means to evaluate a model, best practices for gauging the advocacy of a model, how to split your data, and several considerations that you'll have to make when preparing your split.

It is important to understand some core best practices of machine learning. One of our primary tasks as ML practitioners is to create a model that is effective for making predictions on new data. But how do we know that a model is good? If you recall from the previous section, we defined supervised learning as simply a task that learns a function from labelled data such that we can approximate the target of the new data. Therefore, we can test our model's effectiveness. We can determine how it performs on data that is never seen—just like it's taking a test.

Out-of-sample versus in-sample evaluation

Let's say we are training a small machine which is a simple classification task. Here's some nomenclature you'll need: the in-sample data is the data the model learns from and the out-of-sample data is the data the model has never seen before. One of the pitfalls many new data scientists make is that they measure their model's effectiveness on the same data that the model learned from. What this ends up doing is rewarding the model's ability to memorize, rather than its ability to generalize, which is a huge difference.

If you take a look at the two examples here, the first presents a sample that the model learned from, and we can be reasonably confident that it's going to predict one, which would be correct. The second example presents a new sample, which appears to resemble more of the zero class. Of course, the model doesn't know that. But a good model should be able to recognize and generalize this pattern, shown as follows:

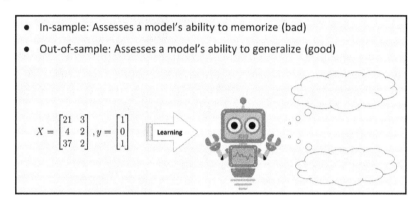

So, now the question is how we can ensure both in-sample and out-of-sample data for the model to prove its worth. Even more precisely, our out-of-sample data needs to be labeled. New or unlabeled data won't suffice because we have to know the actual answer in order to determine how correct the model is. So, one of the ways we can handle this in machine learning is to split our data into two parts: a training set and a testing set. The training set is what our model will learn on; the testing set is what our model will be evaluated on. How much data you have matters a lot. In fact, in the next sections, when we discuss the bias-variance trade-off, you'll see how some models require much more data to learn than others do.

Another thing to keep in mind is that if some of the distributions of your variables are highly skewed, or you have rare categorical levels embedded throughout, or even class imbalance in your y vector, you may end up getting a bad split. As an example, let's say you have a binary feature in your X matrix that indicates the presence of a very rare sensor for some event that occurs every 10,000 occurrences. If you randomly split your data and all of the positive sensor events are in your test set, then your model will learn from the training data that the sensor is never tripped and may deem that as an unimportant variable when, in reality, it could be hugely important, and hugely predictive. So, you can control these types of issues with stratification.

Splitting made easy

Here, we have a simple snippet that demonstrates how we can use the scikit-learn library to split our data into training and test sets. We're loading the data in from the datasets module and passing both X and y into the split function. We should be familiar with loading the data up. We have the `train_test_split` function from the `model_selection` submodule in `sklearn`. This is going to take any number of arrays. So, 20% is going to be `test_size`, and the remaining 80% of that data will be training. We define `random_state`, so that our split can be reproducible if we ever have to prove exactly how we got this split. There's also the `stratify` keyword, which we're not using here, which can be used to `stratify` a split for rare features or an imbalanced y vector:

```
from sklearn.datasets import load_boston

from sklearn.model_selection import train_test_split


boston_housing = load_boston() # load data

X, y = boston_housing.data, boston_housing.target # get X, y

X_train, X_test, y_train, y_test = train_test_split(X, y, test_size=0.2,

random_state=42)

# show num samples (there are no duplicates in either set!)
print("Num train samples: %i" % X_train.shape[0])

print("Num test samples: %i" % X_test.shape[0])
```

The output of the preceding code is as follows:

```
Num train samples: 404
Num test samples: 102
```

Summary

In this chapter, we introduced supervised learning, got our environment put together, and learned about hill climbing and model evaluation. At this point, you should understand the abstract conceptual underpinnings of what makes a machine learn. It's all about optimizing a number of loss functions. In the next chapter, we'll jump into parametric models and even code some popular algorithms from scratch.

2
Implementing Parametric Models

In the previous chapter, we got started with the basics of supervised machine learning. In this chapter, we will dive into the guts of several popular supervised learning algorithms within the parametric modeling family. We'll start this chapter by formally introducing parametric models. Then, we'll introduce two very popular parametric models: linear and logistic regression. We'll spend some time looking at their inner workings and then we'll jump into Python and actually code those workings from scratch.

In this chapter, we will cover the following topics:

- Parametric models
- Implementing linear regression from scratch
- Logistic regression models
- Implementing logistic regression from scratch
- The pros and cons of parametric models

Technical requirements

For this chapter, you will need to install the following software, if you haven't already done so:

- Jupyter Notebook
- Anaconda
- Python

The code files for this chapter can be found at `https://github.com/PacktPublishing/Supervised-Machine-Learning-with-Python`.

Parametric models

When it comes to supervised learning, there are two families of learning algorithms: **parametric** and **non-parametric**. This area also happens to be a hotbed for gatekeeping and opinion-based conjecture regarding which is better. Basically, parametric models are finite-dimensional, which means that they can learn only a defined number of model parameters. Their learning stage is typically categorized by learning some vector theta, which is also called a **coefficient**. Finally, the learning function is often a known form, which we will clarify later in this section.

Finite-dimensional models

If we go back to our definition of supervised learning, recall that we need to learn some function, f. A parametric model will summarize the mapping between X, our matrix, and y, our target, within a constrained number of summary points. The number of points is typically related to the number of features in the input data. So, if there are three variables, f will try to summarize the relationship between X and y given that there are three values in theta. These are called **model parameters** f: $y=f(X)$.

Let's back up and explain some of the characteristics of parametric models.

The characteristics of parametric learning algorithms

We will now cover different features of parametric learning algorithms:

- Model parameters are generally constrained to the same dimensionalities of the input space
- You can point to a variable and its corresponding parameter value and typically learn something about variable importance or its relationship to y, our target
- Finally, they are conventionally fast and do not require much data

Parametric model example

Imagine that we are asked to estimate the price of a house given its square footage and number of bathrooms. How many parameters are we going to need to learn? How many parameters will we have to learn for our example?

Well, given the square footage and number of bathrooms we will have to learn two parameters. So, our function can be expressed as the estimated price given two variables—square footage and the number of bathrooms—*P1* and *P2*. *P1* will be the relationship between square footage and price. *P2* will be the relationship between the number of bathrooms and price.

The following code shows the problem set up in Python. x1 is our first variable—the amount of square footage. You can see that this ranges from anything as small as 1200 to as high as 4000 and our price range is anywhere from 200000 to 500000. In x2, we have the number of bathrooms. This ranges from as few as 1 to as many as 4:

```
import numpy as np
from numpy import linalg

x1 = np.array([2500, 2250, 3500, 4000, 1890, 1200, 2630])
x2 = np.array([3, 2, 4, 3, 2, 1, 2])
y = np.array([260000, 285000, 425000, 482500, 205000, 220000, 320000])
```

Now, you can see from our plots that there seems to be a positive trend going on here. And that makes sense. But we're going to find out as we dig into this example:

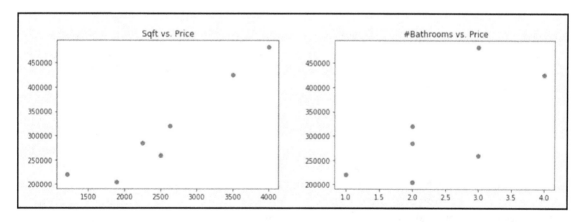

Now, we want to learn a function that estimates the price, and that function is simply going to be the inner product of our estimated parameters in each vector row of our data. So, we are performing linear regression here. Linear regression can conveniently be solved by using the least squares equation. Since we technically have an infinite number of possible solutions to this problem, least squares will find the solution that minimizes the sum of the squared error.

Here, we complete our least squares on X, and learn our parameters in the first cell. Then, in the next cell, we multiply X by the theta parameters that we just learned to get the predictions. So, if you really dig into it, there's only one home that we grossly underestimate in value: the second to last one, which is 1200 square foot and has one bathroom. So, it's probably an apartment and it may be located in a really hot part of town, which is why it was priced so highly to begin with:

```
# solve for the values of theta
from numpy import linalg
X = np.hstack((x1.reshape(x1.shape[0], 1), x2.reshape(x2.shape[0], 1)))
linalg.lstsq(X, y)[0]

# get the estimated y values
X.dot(linalg.lstsq(X,y)[0])
```

The output of the preceding code snippet is as follows:

```
array([   142.58050018, -23629.43252307])

array([285562.95287566, 273547.26035425, 404514.02053054, 499433.70314259,
       222218.28029018, 147467.16769047, 327727.85042187])
```

Now to pick apart our parameters. With each square foot that we add to our house, the estimated price jumps by 142 dollars and 58 cents, which intuitively makes sense. However, for each bathroom we add, our house decreases in value by 24,000 dollars: *Price = 142.58 *sqft + -23629.43*bathrooms.*

There's another conundrum here. By this logic, if we had a house with 3,000 square feet and 0 bathrooms, it would be priced in the ballpark of what a 4,000-square-feet home that has four bathrooms is. So, there's obviously some limitations with our model here. When we try to summarize the mapping with few features and data, there are going to be some non sequiturs that emerge. But there are some other factors that we didn't consider that can help us out when we're fitting our linear regression. First of all, we did not fit an intercept and we did not center our features. So, if you go back to middle school or even early high school algebra, you will remember that, when you're fitting your good line on a Cartesian plot, the intercept is where the line intersects the y axis, and we did not fit one of those.

In the following code, we have centered our data before solving the least squares and estimated an intercept, which is simply the average of y, the actual prices minus the inner product of the X var, which is the means of the columns of X and the estimated parameters:

```
X_means = X.mean(axis=0) # compute column (variable) name
X_center = X - X_means  # center our data
theta = linalg.lstsq(X_center, y)[0]  # solve lstsq
print ("Theta: %r" % theta)

intercept = y.mean() -np.dot(X_means, theta.T) # find the intercept
print("Intercept: %.2f" % intercept)
print("Preds: %r" % (X.dot(theta.T) + intercept))
```

The output of the preceding code snippet is as follows:

```
Theta: array([ 128.90596161, -28362.07260241])
Intercept: 51887.87
Preds: array([289066.55823365, 285202.14043457, 389610.44723722,
482425.50064261,
 238795.99425642, 178212.9533507 , 334186.40584484])
```

So, that summarizes the introduction to the math and the concept behind linear regression, as well as that of parametric learning. In linear regression, we are simply fitting the best line across a number of points, trying to minimize the sum of squared errors there. In the next section, we will learn about PyCharm, and walk through how to actually code a linear regression class from scratch.

Implementing linear regression from scratch

Linear regression solves the least squares equation to discover the parameters vector theta. In this section, we will walk through the source code for a linear regression class in the packtml Python library and then cover a brief graphical example in the examples directory.

Before we look at the code, we will be introduced to the interface that backs all of the estimators in the book. It is called BaseSimpleEstimator, which is an abstract class. It's going to enforce only one method, which is predict. Different subclass layers are going to enforce other methods for different model families. But this layer backs all the models that we will build, as everything that we are putting together is supervised, so it's all going to need to be able to predict. You will notice that the signature is prescribed in the dock string. Every model will accept X and y in the signature, as well as any other model hyperparameters:

```
class BaseSimpleEstimator(six.with_metaclass(ABCMeta)):
    """Base class for packt estimators.
    The estimators in the Packt package do not behave exactly like
    scikit-learn
    estimators (by design). They are made to perform the model fit
    immediately upon class instantiation. Moreover, many of the hyper
    parameter options are limited to promote readability and avoid
    confusion.
    The constructor of every Packt estimator should resemble the
    following::
    def __init__(self, X, y, *args, **kwargs):
    ...
    where ``X`` is the training matrix, ``y`` is the training target
    variable,
    and ``*args`` and ``**kwargs`` are varargs that will differ for each
    estimator.
    """

    @abstractmethod
    def predict(self, X):
    """Form predictions based on new data.
    This function must be implemented by subclasses to generate
    predictions given the model fit.
    Parameters
    ----------
    X : array-like, shape=(n_samples, n_features)
    The test array. Should be only finite values.
    """
```

The BaseSimpleEstimator interface

The first flush is similar to that of a scikit-learn base estimator interface. But there are several differences. First of all, we're not going to permit as many options when we build a model. Furthermore, the model is trained at the moment it's instantiated. This also differs from scikit-learn in the fact that we don't have a `fit` method. Scikit-learn has a `fit` method to permit grid searches and hyperparameter tuning. So, this is just one more reason that we're differing from their signature. With that, let's go ahead and look into linear regression:

1. If you have PyCharm, go ahead and open it up. We are going to be inside the `packtml Hands-on-Supervised-Machine-Learning-with-Python` library, as shown in the following code. You can see this is in PyCharm. This is just the root level of the project level and the package we're going to be working with is `packtml`. We are just going to walk through how all of the `simple_regression.py` file code works. If you are not using PyCharm, Sublime is an alternative, or you can use any other text editor of your preference:

```python
from __future__ import absolute_import

from sklearn.utils.validation import check_X_y, check_array

import numpy as np
from numpy.linalg import lstsq

from packtml.base import BaseSimpleEstimator


__all__ = [
    'SimpleLinearRegression'
]


class SimpleLinearRegression(BaseSimpleEstimator):
    """Simple linear regression.

    This class provides a very simple example of straight forward OLS
    regression with an intercept. There are no tunable parameters, and
    the model fit happens directly on class instantiation.

    Parameters
    ----------
    X : array-like, shape=(n_samples, n_features)
    The array of predictor variables. This is the array we will use
    to regress on ``y``.
```

base.py, which is is located inside our package level, will provide the interface for BaseSimpleEstimator, which we will use across the entire package. The only method that is going to be enforced on the abstract level for everything is the predict function. This function will take one argument, which is X. We already mentioned that supervised learning means that we will learn a function, *f*, given X and y, such that we can approximate $\hat{y}$ given $\hat{X}$, or the X test in this case. Since every subclass is going to implement a different predict method, we will use the abstract method, which is base, as shown in the following code snippet:

```
@abstractmethod
    def predict(self, X):
        """Form predictions based on new data.
        This function must be implemented by subclasses to generate
        predictions given the model fit.
        Parameters
        ----------
        X : array-like, shape=(n_samples, n_features)
        The test array. Should be only finite values.
        """
```

2. Next, inside the regression submodule, we will open the simple_regression.py file. This file will implement a class called SimpleLinearRegression. We call it simple just so you don't confuse it with the scikit-learn linear regression:

```
from __future__ import absolute_import

from sklearn.utils.validation import check_X_y, check_array

import numpy as np
from numpy.linalg import lstsq

from ..base import BaseSimpleEstimator


__all__ = [
    'SimpleLinearRegression'
]


class SimpleLinearRegression(BaseSimpleEstimator):
    """Simple linear regression.

    This class provides a very simple example of straight forward
OLS
```

```
      regression with an intercept. There are no tunable parameters,
and
      the model fit happens directly on class instantiation.

      Parameters
      ----------
      X : array-like, shape=(n_samples, n_features)
          The array of predictor variables. This is the array we will
use
          to regress on ``y``.
```

`SimpleLinearRegression` is going to take two arguments. `X`, which is our matrix covariance, and `y`, the training targets, explained as follows:

```
   Parameters
   ----------
   X : array-like, shape=(n_samples, n_features)
       The array of predictor variables. This is the array we will
use
       to regress on ``y``.

   y : array-like, shape=(n_samples,)
       This is the target array on which we will regress to build
       our model.
   Attributes
   ----------
   theta : array-like, shape=(n_features,)
       The least-squares solution (the coefficients)

   rank : int
       The rank of the predictor matrix, ``X``

   singular_values : array-like, shape=(n_features,)
       The singular values of ``X``

   X_means : array-like, shape=(n_features,)
       The column means of the predictor matrix, ``X``

   y_mean : float
       The mean of the target variable, ``y``

   intercept : float
       The intercept term
   """
   def __init__(self, X, y):
       # First check X, y and make sure they are of equal length,
no
```

```
NaNs
# and that they are numeric
X, y = check_X_y(X, y, y_numeric=True,
                    accept_sparse=False) # keep it simple
```

3. Now, in our signature, the very first thing that we will do inside the `init` function is run this through scikit-learn's `check_X_y`. We will make sure that the dimensionality matches between X and y, as it won't work for us to pass a vector of training targets that is smaller than that of the number of samples in X and vice versa. We are also enforcing that everything that is in y is numeric.

4. The next thing we need to do is compute the mean of the columns in X, so that we can center everything, and the mean of the values in y, so that we can center them. In this entire function, it is from the least squares optimization function that we pulled out of the NumPy library. So, we're just going to feed in X and y, which are now centered in `lstsq`. We will get back three things, the first of which is theta, which is the learned parameter. So, X.theta is going to be the best approximate value of y. We're then going to get the rank, which is the rank of `matrix` and `singular_values`, in case you want to dig into the decomposition of the actual solution. As discussed in the last section, regarding the mean house cost, if we're computing the value of a house minus the inner product of X_means, the column means is a vector times theta, another vector. So, we're going to get a scalar value here for the intercept and we're going to assign some `self` attributes:

```
# We will do the same with our target variable, y
X_means = np.average(X, axis=0)
y_mean = y.mean(axis=0)

# don't do in place, so we get a copy
X = X - X_means
y = y - y_mean

# Let's compute the least squares on X wrt y
# Least squares solves the equation `a x = b` by computing a
# vector `x` that minimizes the Euclidean 2-norm `|| b - a x ||^2`.
theta, _, rank, singular_values = lstsq(X, y, rcond=None)

# finally, we compute the intercept values as the mean of the
target
# variable MINUS the inner product of the X_means and the
coefficients
intercept = y_mean - np.dot(X_means, theta.T)

# ... and set everything as an instance attribute
```

```
self.theta = theta
self.rank = rank
self.singular_values = singular_values

# we have to retain some of the statistics around the data too
self.X_means = X_means
self.y_mean = y_mean
self.intercept = intercept
```

The moment that you instantiate a class, you have fit a linear regression. However, we have to override the `predict` functions from the `BaseSimpleEstimator` superclass. To predict this, all you have to do is compute the inner product of X, the new matrix on `theta`, and the parameters that we've already learned, and then add the intercept. Now, what differs here from what you saw on the constructor is that we don't have to re-center X. If an X test comes in, the only time we center the data is when we're learning the parameters and not when we're applying them. Then, we will multiply X times the parameters, the inner product there, and then add the intercept. Now we have a vector of predicted $\hat{y}$ values:

```
def predict(self, X):
        """Compute new predictions for X"""
        # copy, make sure numeric, etc...
        X = check_array(X, accept_sparse=False, copy=False) # type:
np.ndarray

        # make sure dims match
        theta = self.theta
        if theta.shape[0] != X.shape[1]:
            raise ValueError("Dim mismatch in predictors!")

        # creates a copy
        return np.dot(X, theta.T) + self.intercept
```

5. So, now, we can go ahead and look at one of our examples. Open up the examples directory at the project level, and then open up regression. We will look at the example_linear_regression.py file, as follows:

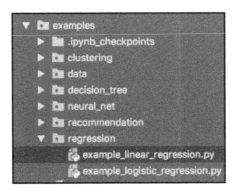

Let's walk through exactly what happens here, just to show you how we can apply this to real data. We will load up the linear regression that we just created and import scikit-learn's linear regression so that we can compare the results. The first thing we're going to do is create the X matrix of random values with 500 samples and 2 dimensions. We will then create the y matrix, which will be a linear combination of the first X variable and 0, which will be 2 times the first column plus 1.5 times the second column. The reason we are doing this is to show that our linear regression class is going to learn these exact parameters, 2 and 1.5, as shown in the following code snippets:

```
from packtml.regression import SimpleLinearRegression
from sklearn.linear_model import LinearRegression
from sklearn.model_selection import train_test_split
from matplotlib import pyplot as plt
import numpy as np
import sys

#
####################################################################
##########
# Create a data-set that perfectly models the linear relationship:
# y = 2a + 1.5b + 0
random_state = np.random.RandomState(42)
X = random_state.rand(500, 2)
y = 2. * X[:, 0] + 1.5 * X[:, 1]
```

As we've already discussed, we want to split our data. You never want to just evaluate and fit against your in-sample data; otherwise, you're prone to overfitting:

```
# split the data
X_train, X_test, y_train, y_test = train_test_split(X, y,

random_state=random_state)
```

6. Next, we will fit our linear regression and compute our predictions. So, we can also show with our assertion that the theta that we learned is incredibly close to the actual theta that we expected; that is, 2 and 1.5. Therefore, our predictions should resemble the y train input:

```
# Fit a simple linear regression, produce predictions
lm = SimpleLinearRegression(X_train, y_train)
predictions = lm.predict(X_test)
print("Test sum of residuals: %.3f" % (y_test - predictions).sum())
assert np.allclose(lm.theta, [2., 1.5])
```

7. Next, we will fit a scikit-learn regression to show that we get a similar result, if not the exact same result. We're showing that the theta in the class that we just created matches the coefficients that scikit-learn produces. Scikit-learn is an incredibly well-tested and well-known library. So, the fact that they match shows that we are on the right track. Finally, we can show that our predictions are very close to the scikit-learn solution:

```
# Show that our solution is similar to scikit-learn's

lr = LinearRegression(fit_intercept=True)
lr.fit(X_train, y_train)
assert np.allclose(lm.theta, lr.coef_)
assert np.allclose(predictions, lr.predict(X_test))
```

8. We will now fit a linear regression on a class, so that we can look at a plot. To do this, let's go ahead and run the following example:

```
# Fit another on ONE feature so we can show the plot
X_train = X_train[:, np.newaxis, 0]
X_test = X_test[:, np.newaxis, 0]
lm = SimpleLinearRegression(X_train, y_train)

# create the predictions & plot them as the line
preds = lm.predict(X_test)
plt.scatter(X_test[:, 0], y_test, color='black')
plt.plot(X_test[:, 0], preds, linewidth=3)

# if we're supposed to save it, do so INSTEAD OF showing it
if len(sys.argv) > 1:
    plt.savefig(sys.argv[1])
else:
    plt.show()
```

9. Go to the Terminal inside the `Hands-on-Supervised-Machine-Learning-with-Python-master` top level: the project level. Remember to source the content environment. So, if you've not already done that, you will need to `source activate` for Unix users, or just activate by typing the following:

   source activate packt-sml

10. Run this example by typing the name of the file, which is `examples/regression/example_linear_regression.py`:

```
test@test-Veriton-Series:~/Documents/Hands-on-Supervised-Machine-Learning-with-Python-master$ source activate packt-sml
(packt-sml) test@test-Veriton-Series:~/Documents/Hands-on-Supervised-Machine-Learning-with-Python-master$ python examples/regression
example_linear_regression.p
y
/home/test/anaconda3/envs/packt-sml/lib/python3.6/site-packages/packtml-1.0.3-py3.6.egg/packtml/regression/simple_regression.py:73: F
utureWarning: `rcond` parameter will change to the default of machine precision times `max(M, N)` where M and N are the input matri
x dimensions.
To use the future default and silence this warning we advise to pass `rcond=None`, to keep using the old, explicitly pass `rcond=-1`.
  theta, _, rank, singular_values = lstsq(X, y)
Test sum of residuals: -0.000
```

When we run the preceding code, we should get our plot, as shown in the following screenshot:

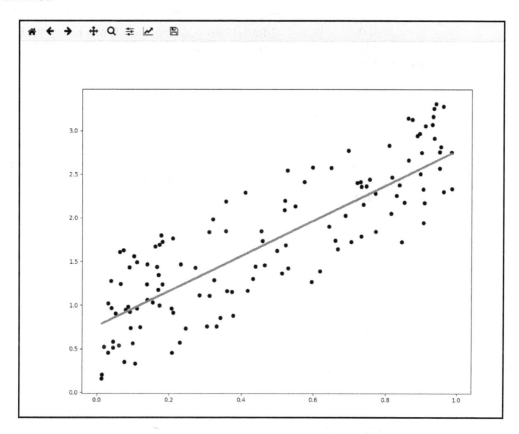

We can see that our sum of residuals is essentially zero, meaning that we were spot on in our predictions. It is easy in this case, because we created a scenario where we learned our exact theta values. You can see here the line that we're fitting across one variable. This is a bit more approximated given that we only learned it on one variable. It seems to both qualitatively and quantitatively match what we expected via scikit-learn's predictions and coefficients.

In the next section, we will learn about logistic regression models.

Logistic regression models

In this section, we will look at logistic regression, which is the first hill-climbing algorithm that we'll cover, and we will have a brief recap of linear regression. We will also look at how logistic regression differs both mathematically and conceptually. Finally, we will learn the core algorithm and explain how it makes predictions.

The concept

Logistic regression is conceptually the inverse of linear regression. What if, rather than a real value, we want a discrete value or a class? We have already seen one example of this type of question early on when we wanted to predict whether or not an email was spam. So, with logistic regression, rather than predicting a real value, we can predict the probability of class membership, also known as classification.

The math

Mathematically, logistic regression is very similar to linear regression. The inner product of our parameters and X represent the log odds of the membership of a class, which is simply the natural log of the probabilities over *1* minus the probabilities:

$$logit(p) = \ln\left(\frac{p}{1-p}\right) = \theta^T X$$

What we really want are the probabilities of the class membership. We can back out of the log odds and determine the probabilities using the sigmoid or logistic function.

The logistic (sigmoid) transformation

In the following code, we will create an X vector of values between -10 and 10 and then apply the logistic transformation to get y, which we can then plot:

```
import numpy as np
import matplotlib.pyplot as plt
%matplotlib inline

x = np.linspace(-10, 10, 10000)
y = 1. / (1 + np.exp(-x)) # sigmoid transformation
plt.plot(x, y)
```

As you can see, we get an S-shaped curve with the original X values on the x axis and the y values on the y axis. Notice that everything is mapped between zero and one on the y axis. These can now be interpreted as probabilities:

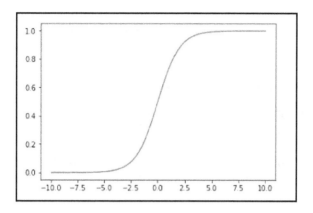

The algorithm

Now, we have already covered the logistic regression algorithm briefly in the earlier section. But here's a recap of how we learn our parameters:

1. We start out by initializing theta as a zero vector:

$$\theta = \overrightarrow{0^n}$$

2. As this is a hill-climbing algorithm, it is iterative. So, for each iteration, we compute the log odds as theta transpose X and then transform them via the logistic transformation:

$$\hat{y} = \frac{1}{1 + e^{-(\theta^T X)}}$$

3. Next, we compute the gradient, which is a vector of partial derivatives of the slope of our function, which we covered in the last section. We simply compute this as X transpose times the residuals, y - $\hat{y}$. Keep in mind that $\hat{y}$ is the probability now following the logistic transformation:

$$X^T(y - \hat{y})$$

4. Finally, we can update our coefficients as theta plus the gradient. You can also see a λ parameter here, which is simply a learning rate parameter. This controls how radically we allow the coefficients to grow for each step:

$$\theta = \theta + \lambda(X^T(\hat{y} - y))$$

Creating predictions

We finally converge our gradient, which is no longer updating our coefficients, and we are left with a bunch of class probabilities. So, how do we produce the predictions? All we have to do is get above a given threshold and we can get classes. So, in this section, we will be using a binary problem. But, for multi-class, we could just use the argmax functions for each class. Now, we will produce discrete predictions, as shown in the following code:

```
sigmoid = (lambda x: 1. / (1 + np.exp(-x)))
log_odds = np.array([-5.6, 8.9, 3.7, 0.6, 0.])
probas = sigmoid(log_odds)
classes = np.round(probas).astype(int)
print("Log odds: %r\nProbas: %r\nClasses: %r"
      % (log_odds, probas, classes))
```

The output of the preceding code is as follows:

```
Log odds: array([-5.6, 8.9, 3.7, 0.6, 0. ])
Probas: array([0.00368424, 0.99986363, 0.97587298, 0.64565631, 0.5 ])
Classes: array([0, 1, 1, 1, 0])
```

In the next section, we will walk through the implementation of logistic regression from scratch in the `packtml` package.

Implementing logistic regression from scratch

In this section, we will walk through the implementation of logistic regression in Python within the `packtml` package. We will start off with a brief recap of what logistic regression seeks to accomplish and then go over the source code and look at an example.

Recall that logistic regression seeks to classify a sample into a discrete category, also known as **classification**. The logistic transformation allows us to transform the log odds that we get from the inner product of our parameters and X.

Notice that we have three Python files open. One is extmath.py, from within the utils directory inside of packtml; another is simple_logistic.py, from within the regression library in packtml; and the final one is an example_logistic_regression.py file, inside the examples directory and regression.

We will dive right into the code base using the following steps:

1. We will start with the extmath.py file. There are two functions that we will be using here. The first is log_likelihood, which is the objective function that we would like to maximize inside of the logistic regression:

```
def log_likelihood(X, y, w):
    """Compute the log-likelihood function.

    Computes the log-likelihood function over the training data.
    The key to the log-likelihood is that the log of the product of
    likelihoods becomes the sum of logs. That is (in pseudo-code),

        np.log(np.product([f(i) for i in range(N)]))

    is equivalent to:

        np.sum([np.log(f(i)) for i in range(N)])

    The log-likelihood function is used in computing the gradient
for
    our loss function since the derivative of the sum (of logs) is
equivalent
    to the sum of derivatives, which simplifies all of our math.
```

2. The specifics of the log_likelihood function are not necessarily critical for understanding how logistic regression works. But, essentially, what you can see here is that we will be summing up y times the log odds, minus the log of 1 plus the exponential of the log odds. Weighted here is essentially the log odds, that is, X.dot(w), w being the theta that we are learning. This is the objective function. So, we're summing over those logs:

```
weighted = X.dot(w)
return (y * weighted - np.log(1. + np.exp(weighted))).sum()
```

3. The second is the `logistic_sigmoid` function, which we will now learn in greater depth. This is how we can back out of the log odds to get the class probabilities, which is simply 1 over 1 plus the exponential of the negative log odds, where x is the log odds in this case:

```
def logistic_sigmoid(x):
    """The logistic function.

    Compute the logistic (sigmoid) function over a vector, ``x``.

    Parameters
    ----------
    x : np.ndarray, shape=(n_samples,)
        A vector to transform.
    """
    return 1. / (1. + np.exp(-x))
```

4. We will use both of these functions inside the logistic regression class. So, inside of `simple_logistic.py`, you will see a class that resembles the linear regression class that we used in the last section:

```
# -*- coding: utf-8 -*-

from __future__ import absolute_import

from sklearn.utils.validation import check_X_y, check_array

import numpy as np
from packtml.utils.extmath import log_likelihood, logistic_sigmoid
from packtml.utils.validation import assert_is_binary
from packtml.base import BaseSimpleEstimator

__all__ = [
    'SimpleLogisticRegression'
]

try:
    xrange
except NameError: # py 3 doesn't have an xrange
    xrange = range


class SimpleLogisticRegression(BaseSimpleEstimator):
    """Simple logistic regression.

    This class provides a very simple example of straight forward
logistic
```

```
      regression with an intercept. There are few tunable parameters
aside from
      the number of iterations, & learning rate, and the model is fit
upon
      class initialization.
```

5. Now, this function, or class, extends `BaseSimpleEstimator`. We will override the `predict` function at some point and the constructor will fit the model and learn the parameters. So, we have four hyperparameters here that come in for this class. The first of which is `X`, which is our training data; then `y`, as our training labels; and `n_steps` recalls that logistic regression as an iterative model. So, `n_steps` is the number of iterations that we will perform to which the `learning_rate` is our lambda. If you go back to the algorithm itself, this controls how quickly we update our theta given the gradients, and, lastly, `loglik_interval`. This is just a helper parameter. Computing the log likelihood can be pretty expensive. We can see this explanation in the following code snippet:

```
Parameters
----------
X : array-like, shape=(n_samples, n_features)
        The array of predictor variables. This is the array we will
use
        to regress on ``y``.

y : array-like, shape=(n_samples,)
        This is the target array on which we will regress to build
        our model. It should be binary (0, 1).

n_steps : int, optional (default=100)
        The number of iterations to perform.

learning_rate : float, optional (default=0.001)
        The learning rate.

loglik_interval : int, optional (default=5)
        How frequently to compute the log likelihood. This is an
expensive
        operation--computing too frequently will be very expensive.
```

6. At the end, we get `theta`, the parameters, `intercept`, and then `log_likelihood`, which is just a list of the computed log likelihoods at each of the intervals. We will first check that our X and y are as we want them to be, which is 0, 1. We won't do anything close to what scikit-learn is capable of. We will also not allow different string classes either:

```
def __init__(self, X, y, n_steps=100, learning_rate=0.001,
                loglik_interval=5):
        X, y = check_X_y(X, y, accept_sparse=False, # keep dense
for example
                            y_numeric=True)

        # we want to make sure y is binary since that's all our
example covers
        assert_is_binary(y)

        # X should be centered/scaled for logistic regression, much
like
        # with linear regression
        means, stds = X.mean(axis=0), X.std(axis=0)
        X = (X - means) / stds
```

7. Next, we want to make sure that it's actually binary. The reason for this is that we're performing logistic regression, which is discrete between 0 and 1. There is a generalization of the regression, called **softmax regression**, which will allow us to use a number of different classes. it's a multi-class classification. We will get to this when we get into neural nets. For now, we're constraining this to be a binary problem.

8. Next, we want to center and standardize our X matrix. That means we're going to subtract the column `means` from X and divide it by its standard deviation. So, we have mean 0, and standard deviation 1:

```
# since we're going to learn an intercept, we can cheat and set the
# intercept to be a new feature that we'll learn with everything
else
X_w_intercept = np.hstack((np.ones((X.shape[0], 1)), X))
```

9. Now, we can do something a little bit clever here when we are learning our linear regression parameters, or the logistic regression parameters that we could not do in linear regression. We can add the intercept to the matrix while we learn it, rather than having to compute it after the fact. We will create a vector of ones as a new feature on our X matrix, as shown:

```
# initialize the coefficients as zeros
theta = np.zeros(X_w_intercept.shape[1])
```

10. As we defined in our algorithm, we start out by defining that theta is equal to zero. There are as many parameters as there are columns in X. For each iteration, we will compute the log odds here. Then, we transform this with a logistic sigmoid. We will compute our residuals as `y - preds`. So, at this point, `preds` is probabilities. `y` can be considered to be class probabilities for a binary classification problem where `1` is 100% probable that something belongs to class `1`, and `0` is 0% probable that something belongs to class `1`:

```
# now for each step, we compute the inner product of X and the
# coefficients, transform the predictions with the sigmoid
function,
# and adjust the weights by the gradient
ll = []
for iteration in xrange(n_steps):
    preds = logistic_sigmoid(X_w_intercept.dot(theta))
    residuals = y - preds # The error term
    gradient = X_w_intercept.T.dot(residuals)
```

So, we can subtract the probabilities from `y` to get our residuals. In order to get our gradient, we will perform X times the residuals, which is the inner product there. Keep in mind that a gradient is a vector of partial derivatives for the slope of our function.

11. We will update `theta` and the parameters by adding the gradient times our learning rate. The learning rate is the lambda function that controls how quickly we learn. As you may remember, if we learn too quickly, we can overstep a global optimum and end up getting a non-optimal solution. If we go too slowly, then we're going to fit for a long time. Logistic regression is an interesting case; as this is actually a convex optimization problem, we will have enough iterations to reach the global optimum. So, `learning_rate` here is a little bit tongue-in-cheek, but this is how, in general, hill-climbing functions work by using `learning_rate`:

```
# update the coefficients
theta += learning_rate * gradient

# you may not always want to do this, since it's expensive. Tune
# the error_interval to increase/reduce this
if (iteration + 1) % loglik_interval == 0:
    ll.append(log_likelihood(X_w_intercept, y, theta))
```

12. The very last step here is that, if we are at the proper intervals, we will compute `log_likelihood`. Now, again, you could compute this function at every iteration, but it would take you a very long time. We can opt to make this happen after every 5 or 10 minutes, which will allow us to see that we're optimizing this function. But, at the same time, it means that we don't have to compute it at every iteration.

13. Finally, we will save all of these as instance parameters for a class. Notice that we are stripping out the intercept and keeping 1 onward as far as the parameters go. These are the non-intercept parameters that we'll just compute in our inner product for the predictions:

```
# recall that our theta includes the intercept, so we need to pop
# that off and store it
self.intercept = theta[0]
self.theta = theta[1:]
self.log_likelihood = ll
self.column_means = means
self.column_std = stds
```

So, we take the logistic transformation of X times `theta.T` and then add in `intercept` after we have centered and standardized our input, X, which would then give us the probabilities:

```
# scale the data appropriately
X = (X - self.column_means) / self.column_std

# creates a copy
return logistic_sigmoid(np.dot(X, theta.T) + self.intercept)
```

But, to get the actual prediction, we just round up the probabilities. So, in the `predict` function, we will take `predict_proba` and round it up or down to either zero or one and get the type as `int`, which will give us our classes zero and one:

```
def predict(self, X):
    return np.round(self.predict_proba(X)).astype(int)
```

Example of logistic regression

Now, as an example, we will look at our `example_logistic_regression.py` script. We will compare the output of our `simple_logistic_regression.py` file with that of scikit-learn and prove that we get similar, if not exactly equal, parameters learned in our output. We use the scikit-learn `make_classification` function to create 100 samples and two features and do `train_test_split`. First, we will fit our own `SimpleLogisticRegression` with the model that we just walked through and take 50 steps, as this is a 50 iteration, as shown in the following code:

```
# -*- coding: utf-8 -*-

from __future__ import absolute_import

from packtml.regression import SimpleLogisticRegression
from packtml.utils.plotting import add_decision_boundary_to_axis
from sklearn.linear_model import LogisticRegression
from sklearn.datasets import make_classification
from sklearn.model_selection import train_test_split
from sklearn.metrics import accuracy_score
from matplotlib import pyplot as plt
import sys

#
###############################################################################
##
# Create an almost perfectly linearly-separable classification set
X, y = make_classification(n_samples=100, n_features=2, random_state=42,
                           n_redundant=0, n_repeated=0, n_classes=2,
                           class_sep=1.0)

# split data
X_train, X_test, y_train, y_test = train_test_split(X, y, random_state=42)

#
###############################################################################
##
# Fit a simple logistic regression, produce predictions
lm = SimpleLogisticRegression(X_train, y_train, n_steps=50)

predictions = lm.predict(X_test)
acc = accuracy_score(y_test, predictions)
print("Test accuracy: %.3f" % acc)
```

Next, we will compute scikit-learn's `LogisticRegression` with almost no regularization and fit it as shown:

```
# Show that our solution is similar to scikit-learn's
lr = LogisticRegression(fit_intercept=True, C=1e16) # almost no
regularization
lr.fit(X_train, y_train)
print("Sklearn test accuracy: %.3f" % accuracy_score(y_test,
                                        lr.predict(X_test)))
```

We will run this code. Make sure that you've got your Anaconda environment already activated by typing `source activate packt-sml`.

> If you're on Windows, this would just be `activate packt-sml`.

We see that our test accuracy is 96%, which is pretty close to `Sklearn` at 100%. Scikit-learn runs more iterations, which is why it gets better accuracy. If we ran more iterations, we could theoretically get perfect accuracy. In the following output, you can see a perfectly linearly separable boundary here. But, since we haven't run as many iterations, we're not hitting it. So, what you can see in this diagram is that we have this linear boundary, which is the decision function we've learned, separating these two classes. On the left, you have one class, and on the right, you have another, as shown:

```
(packt-sml) test@test-Veriton-Series:~/Documents/Hands-on-Supervised-Machine-Learning-with-Python-master$ python examples/regression/
example_logistic_regression.py
Test accuracy: 0.960
/home/test/anaconda3/envs/packt-sml/lib/python3.6/site-packages/sklearn/linear_model/logistic.py:433: FutureWarning: Default solver w
ill be changed to 'lbfgs' in 0.22. Specify a solver to silence this warning.
  FutureWarning)
Sklearn test accuracy: 1.000
```

The output of the preceding code is as follows:

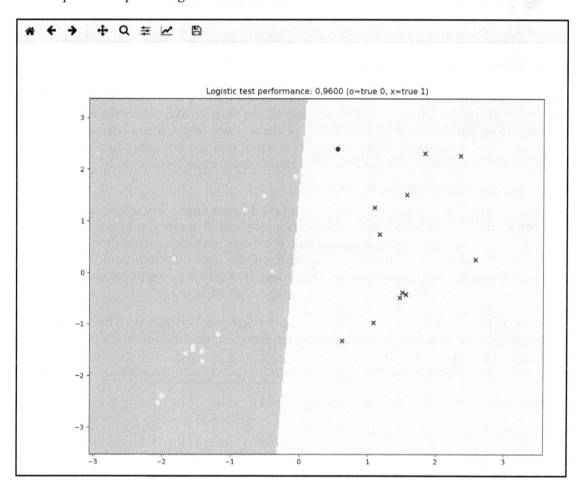

Hypothetically, if we ran this code for a hundred or even more iterations, we could achieve a perfectly linearly separable plane, which could guarantee a linearly separable class, because logistic regression will always reach a global optimum. We also know that our formulation is exactly the same as scikit-learn's. So, it's just a matter of how many iterations we ran there.

In the next section, we're going to look at some of the pros and cons of parametric models.

The pros and cons of parametric models

Parametric models have some really convenient attributes. Namely, they are fast to fit, don't require too much data, and can be very easily explained. In the case of linear and logistic regression, it's easy to look at coefficients and directly explain the impact of fluctuating one variable in either direction. In regulated industries, such as finance or insurance, parametric models tend to reign supreme, since they can be easily explained to regulators. Business partners tend to really rely on the insights that the coefficients produce. However, as is evident in what we've already seen so far, they tend to oversimplify. So, as an example, the logistic regression decision boundary that we looked at in the last section assumes a perfect linear boundary between two classes.

It is rare that the real world can be constrained into linear relationships. That said, the models are very simple. They don't always capture the true nuances of relationships between variables, which is a bit of a double-edged sword. Also, they're heavily impacted by outliers and data scale. So, you have to take great care with data preparation. This is one of the reasons that we had to make sure we centered and scaled our data before fitting. Finally, if you add data to your models, it's unlikely that they're going to get much better. This introduces a new concept, which we're going to call bias.

Error due to bias is a concept we will talk about in subsequent chapters. It's the result of a model that is oversimplified. In the following diagram, our model oversimplifies a `logit` function by treating it as linear:

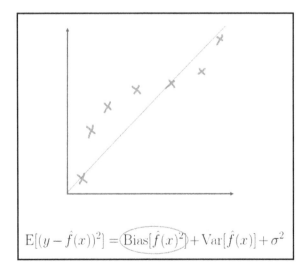

$$E[(y - \hat{f}(x))^2] = \text{Bias}[\hat{f}(x)^2] + \text{Var}[\hat{f}(x)] + \sigma^2$$

This is also known as **underfitting**, which is common within the parametric model family. There are several ways to combat high bias, most of which we will introduce in the next chapter. But, in the spirit of exploring the drawbacks of parametric models, it's worth pointing some of them out here. As mentioned before, we cannot add more data to learn a better function in high-bias situations. If we take the previous example, if you were to add more samples along the logit line, our learned or blue line would not approach the true function any more than it already has, because it's linear. It's not complex enough to model the true underlying function, which is an unfortunate consequence of the simplicity of many parametric models. More model complexity and complex nonlinear features usually help to correct high bias.

Summary

In this chapter, we were introduced to parametric models. We then walked through the low-level math of linear logistic regression, before moving on to implementations in Python. Now that we've covered some of the pros and cons of parametric models, in the next chapter, we will take a look at some non-parametric models.

3
Working with Non-Parametric Models

In the last chapter, we introduced parametric models and explored how to implement linear and logistic regression. In this chapter, we will cover the non-parametric model family. We will start by covering the bias-variance trade-off, and explaining how parametric and non-parametric models differ at a fundamental level. Later, we'll get into decision trees and clustering methods. Finally, we'll address some of the pros and cons of the non-parametric models.

In this chapter, we will cover the following topics:

- The bias/variance trade-off
- An introduction to non-parametric models and decision trees
- Decision trees
- Implementing a decision tree from scratch
- Various clustering methods
- Implementing **K-Nearest Neighbors** (**KNNs**) from scratch
- Non-parametric models – the pros and cons

Technical requirements

For this chapter, you will need to install the following software, if you haven't already done so:

- Jupyter Notebook
- Anaconda
- Python

The code files for this chapter can be found at `https://github.com/PacktPublishing/` `Supervised-Machine-Learning-with-Python`.

The bias/variance trade-off

In this section, we're going to continue our discussion of error due to **bias**, and introduce a new source of error called **variance**. We will begin by clarifying what we mean by error terms and then dissect various sources of modeling errors.

Error terms

One of the central topics of model building is reducing error. However, there are several types of errors, two of which we have control over to some extent. These are called **bias** and **variance**. There is a trade-off in the ability for a model to minimize either bias or variance, and this is called the **bias-variance trade-off** or the **bias-variance dilemma**.

Some models do well at controlling both to an extent. However, this is a dilemma that, for the most part, is always going to be present in your modeling considerations.

Error due to bias

High bias can also be called underfitting or over-generalization. High bias generally leads to an inflexible model that misses the true relationship between features in the target function that we are modeling. In the following diagram, the true relationship between x and y is oversimplified and the true function of $f(x)$, which is essentially a logic function, is missed:

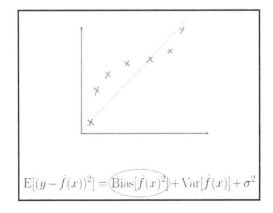

$$E[(y - \hat{f}(x))^2] = \mathrm{Bias}[\hat{f}(x)^2] + \mathrm{Var}[\hat{f}(x)] + \sigma^2$$

Parametric models tend to suffer high bias problems more than non-parametric models. Examples of this include linear and logistic regression, which we will explore in more detail in the final section of this chapter.

Error due to variance

In contrast, for the high bias that you're now familiar with, error due to variance can be thought of as the variability of a model's prediction for a given sample. Imagine you repeat the modeling process many times; the variance is how much the predictions for a given sample will vary across different inductions of the model. High variance models are commonly referred to as overfitting, and suffer the exact inverse of high bias. That is, they do not generalize enough. High variance usually comes from a model's insensitivity to the signal as a result of its hypersensitivity to noise. Generally, as model complexity increases, variance becomes our primary concern. Notice in the diagram that a polynomial term has led to a very overfitting model, where a simple **logit** function would have sufficed:

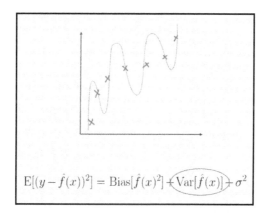

Unlike high bias problems, high variance problems can be addressed with more training data, which can help the model learn to generalize a bit better. So, examples of high variance models, which we haven't yet covered, are decision trees and KNN. We're going to cover both of these in this chapter.

Learning curves

In this section, we will examine a handy way to diagnose high bias or variance called **learning curves**. In this example Python snippet, we will leverage the function in the `packtml.utils` submodule called `plot_learning_curve`, as shown in the following code:

```
from sklearn.datasets import load_boston
from sklearn.metrics import mean_squared_error
from packtml.utils.plotting import plot_learning_curve
from packtml.regression import SimpleLinearRegression
%matplotlib inline

boston = load_boston()
plot_learning_curve(
        model=SimpleLinearRegression, X=boston.data, y=boston.target,
        metric=mean_squared_error, n_folds=3,
        train_sizes=(50, 150, 250, 300),
        seed=42, y_lim=(0, 45))\
    .show
```

This function is going to take an estimator and fit it on various sizes of training data defined in the `train_sizes` parameter. What is displayed is the model performance on the train and the corresponding validation set for each incremental model fit. So, this example uses our linear regression class to model the Boston housing data, which is a regression problem and displays symptoms of high bias. Notice that our error is very similar for the training and validation sets. It got very rapidly, but it's still relatively high. They don't improve as our training set grows at all. We get the output for the preceding code as follows:

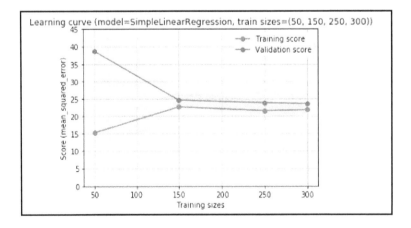

Alternatively, if we model the same data with a decision tree regressor, we notice the symptoms of high variance or overfitting:

```
from sklearn.datasets import load_boston
from sklearn.metrics import mean_squared_error
from packtml.utils.plotting import plot_learning_curve
from packtml.decision_tree import CARTRegressor
%matplotlib inline

boston = load_boston()
plot_learning_curve(
        model=CARTRegressor, X=boston.data, y=boston.target,
        metric=mean_squared_error, n_folds=3,
        train_sizes=(25, 150, 225, 350),
        seed=42, random_state=21, max_depth=50)\
    .show
```

There is a huge discrepancy between the **Training score** and **Validation score**, and even though it gets better with more data, it never quite reaches convergence. We get the following output:

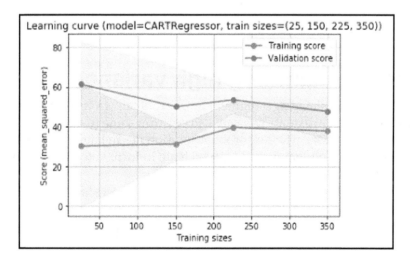

Strategies for handling high bias

If you determine that you're suffering from a high bias problem, you can try making your model more complex by engineering more informative signal-rich features. For example, here, one thing you could try doing is creating new features that are polynomial combinations of your *x1* so, you can create logit function of *x1*, and that would model our function perfectly. You can also try tuning some of the hyperparameters, for instance, KNNs, even though it's a high variance model, and it can become highly biased very quickly as you increase the k hyperparameter, and vice versa:

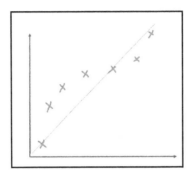

Strategies for handling high variance

If you, instead, find yourself facing a high variance problem, we've already seen how more training data can help, to an extent. You can also perform some feature selection to pare down the model's complexity. The most robust solution lies in bagging or ensembling, which combines the output to mini models, which all, in turn, vote on each sample's label or output regression score:

In the next section, we're going to more formally define non-parametric learning algorithms and introduce decision trees.

Introduction to non-parametric models and decision trees

In this section, we're going to formally define what non-parametric learning algorithms are, and introduce some of the concepts and math behind our first algorithm, called **decision trees**.

Non-parametric learning

Non-parametric models do not learn parameters. They do learn characteristics or attributes about the data, but not parameters in the formal sense. We will not end up extracting a vector of coefficients. The easiest example is a decision tree. A decision tree is going to learn where to recursively split data so that its leaves are as pure as possible. So, in that sense, the decision function is a splitting point for each leaf that is not a parameter.

Characteristics of non-parametric learning algorithms

Non-parametric models tend to be a bit more flexible and do not make as many assumptions about the underlying structure of the data. Many linear models, or parametric models, for instance, assume that a normal distribution for each feature is required to be independent of one another. This is not the case with most non-parametric models. As we covered in the last section, the bias-variance trade-off also knows that non-parametric models will require more data to train, so as not to be as afflicted by high variance problems.

Is a model parametric or not?

If you find yourself wondering whether or not a model is parametric, it's probably not the most important question to answer. You should select the modeling technique that best suits your data. However, a good rule of thumb is how many characteristics or parameters a model learns. If it's related to the feature space or dimensionality, it's probably parametric, for instance, learning the number of coefficients theta in a linear regression. If, instead, it's related to the number of samples, it's probably non-parametric, for instance, the depth of the decision tree or the number of neighbors in clustering.

An intuitive example – decision tree

A decision tree will start out with all of the data, iteratively making splits until each leaf has maximized its purity or some other stopping criteria is met. In this example, we will start out with three samples. The tree learns that splitting on the color feature will be our most informative step towards maximizing its leaf purity. So, that's the first thing to note. The first split is the most informative split that will best segment the data into two pieces. As shown in the following diagram, the potato class is isolated on the left by splitting on color. We have perfectly classified the potato. However, the other two samples still need to be split. So, the tree learns that, if it's orange and round, it's a sweet potato. Otherwise, if it's just orange and not round, it's a carrot, and it goes left one more time. Here, we can see a perfect split of all of our classes:

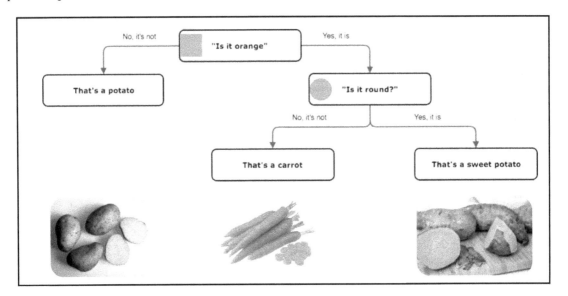

Decision trees – an introduction

What we're interested in doing with decision trees is defining a flexible extensible algorithm that can achieve the decision tree. This is where the **Classification and Regression Trees (CART)** algorithm comes in. CART is generalizable to either task and it learns, essentially, by asking questions of the data. At each split point, CART will scan the entire feature space, sampling values from each feature to identify the best feature and value for the split. It does this by evaluating the information gain formula, which seeks to maximize a gain in purity in the split, which is pretty intuitive. *Gini Impurity* is computed at the leaf level, and is a way of measuring how pure or impure a leaf is; its formula is as follows:

$$GiniImpurity : I_G(p) = 1 - \sum_{i=1}^{J} p_i^2$$

IG at the bottom is our information gain, and it's the gini of the root node, as shown here:

$$IG = I_G(S) - Pr(t)I_G(S|t) - (1 - Pr(t))I_G(S|f)$$

How do decision trees make decisions?

We will first address the objective before looking at the math. We will compute the information gain of a split to determine the best splitting point. If information gain is positive, that means we have learned something from that split, which might be the optimal point. If information gain is negative, it means we're actually going in the wrong direction. What we have done is created a non-informative split. Each split in the tree will select the point that maximizes information gain.

So, here's the setup:

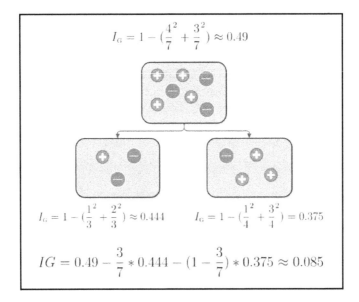

A Gini impurity of 0 would be particularly pure. A higher impurity essentially means that a more random collection of classes has found itself in that leaf. So, our root is fairly impure. Now our tree will scan the entire feature space, sampling values from each feature. It will evaluate the information gained on if we were to split there. So, let's say that our tree selects *x12*. We will split along the same value that's sampled that variable. What we want to know is, if we end up getting more pure leaf nodes from this split, we will compute the information gain. To do that, we have to compute the Gini for each of the leaf nodes that we just created.

We will look at an example of this problem using the `packtml` library. We have the `example_information_gain.py` file, which is in the `examples/decision_tree` directory:

```
# -*- coding: utf-8 -*-

from __future__ import absolute_import

from packtml.decision_tree.metrics import gini_impurity, InformationGain
import numpy as np

#
###################################################################################
##
# Build the example from the slides
```

```
y = np.array([0, 0, 0, 1, 1, 1, 1])
uncertainty = gini_impurity(y)
print("Initial gini impurity: %.4f" % uncertainty)

# now get the information gain of the split from the slides
directions = np.array(["right", "left", "left", "left",
                       "right", "right", "right"])
mask = directions == "left"
print("Information gain from the split we created: %.4f"
      % InformationGain("gini")(target=y, mask=mask,
uncertainty=uncertainty))
```

Next, we will compute the information gain using the `InformationGain` class from
`packtml.decision_tree.metrics`:

```
from packtml.decision_tree.metrics import gini_impurity, InformationGain
import numpy as np
```

We will get the following output when we run `example_information_gain.py`:

```
(packt-sml) test@test-Veriton-Series:~/Documents/Hands-on-Supervised-Machine-Learning-with-Python-master/examples/decision_tree$ pyth
on example_information_gain.py
Initial gini impurity: 0.4898
Information gain from the split we created: 0.0850
```

In the next section, we're going to go a bit deeper and learn how a decision tree produces
the candidate split for us to evaluate.

Decision trees

In the previous section, we computed the information gained for a given split. Recall that
it's computed or calculated by computing the Gini impurity for the parent node in each
`LeafNode`. A higher information again is better, which means we have successfully
reduced the impurities of the child nodes with our split. However, we need to know how a
candidate split is produced to be evaluated.

For each split, beginning with the root, the algorithm will scan all the features in the data,
selecting a random number of values for each. There are various strategies to select these
values. For the general use case, we will describe and select a *k* random approach:

- For each of the sample values in each feature, we simulate a candidate split
- Values above the sampled value go to one direction, say left, and values above
  that go the other direction, that is, to the right

- Now, for each candidate split, we're going to compute the information gain, and select the feature value combination that produces the highest information gain, which is the best split
- From the best split, we will recurse down each split as a new parent until the stopping criteria are met

Now, regarding where and when to stop the criteria, there are various methods we can use for this. A common one is maximum tree depth. If we get too deep, we start to overfit. So, we might prune our tree when it grows five times deep, for instance. Another, is a minimum number of samples per leaf. If we have 1 million training samples, we grow our tree until there's one sample per leaf; we're also probably overfitting. So, the min samples leaf parameter will allow us to stop splitting a leaf once there are, say, 50 samples remaining after a split. This is a tunable hyperparameter that you can work within your cross-validation procedure.

Splitting a tree by hand

We will now look into an exercise. Let's imagine we have this training set:

$$X = \begin{bmatrix} 21 & 3 \\ 4 & 2 \\ 35 & 2 \end{bmatrix}, y = \begin{bmatrix} 1 \\ 0 \\ 1 \end{bmatrix}$$

From the preceding data, where is the optimal split point? What feature or value combination should we use to define our rule?

If we split on x1

First, we will compute the Gini impurity of the root node, which is the pre-split state. We get *0.444*, as shown:

$$Pre - split\ gini\ impurity : I_G = 1 - \left(\frac{1^2}{3} + \frac{2^2}{3}\right) \approx 0.444$$

The next stage in the algorithm is to iterate each feature. There are three cases, shown as follows. Using our *IG* formula, we can compute which is the best split point for this feature. The first happens to be the best, in this case:

$$Split where >= 21$$
$$IG = 0.444 - \tfrac{2}{3} * 0 - (1 - \tfrac{2}{3}) * 0 = 0.444$$

Splitting on the second case, where *x1* is greater than or equal to 4, is not a good idea since the result is no different than the state at the root. Therefore, our information gain is *0*:

$$Split\ where\ >= 21$$
$$IG = 0.444 - \tfrac{2}{3} * 0 - (1 - \tfrac{2}{3}) * 0 = 0.444$$

In the last case, splitting when *x1* is greater than or equal to *37* does yield a positive IG since we have successfully split one sample of the positive class away from the others:

$$Split\ where\ >= 37$$
$$IG = 0.444 - \tfrac{1}{3} * 0 - (1 - \tfrac{1}{3}) * 0.5 \approx 0.111$$

If we split on x2

However, we don't know if we're done yet. So, we will iterate to *x2*, where there might be a better split point:

$$Pre - split\ gini\ impurity = I_G = 1 - (\tfrac{1^2}{3} + \tfrac{2^2}{3}) \approx 0.444$$
$$Split\ where\ >= 3 \quad IG = 0.444 - \tfrac{1}{3} * 0 - (1 - \tfrac{1}{3}) * 0.5 \approx 0.111$$
$$Split\ where\ >= 2 \quad IG = 0.444 - \tfrac{3}{3} * 0.444 - (1 - \tfrac{3}{3}) * 1 = 0$$

The candidate split shows us that neither potential split is the optimal split when compared to the current best that we've identified in *x1*.

Therefore, the best split is *x1* greater than or equal to *21*, which will perfectly separate our class labels. You can see in this decision tree when we produce that split, sure enough, we get perfectly separated classes:

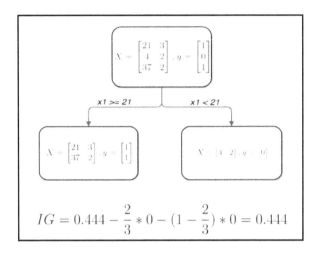

However, in a larger example, we may not have perfectly separated our classes, if we had millions of samples, for instance. Hence, we would recurse at this point, finding new split points for each node until we hit our stopping criteria. At this point, let's use our `packtml` library to run this exact example and show that we do in fact identify the same optimal split point, and prove that is not just trickery of the hand.

In PyCharm, the `example_classification_split.py` file is open. This is located inside your `examples` directory and within the `decision_tree` examples directory. You can see we're going to import two things from `packtml`. Both of them happen to be inside the `decision_tree` submodule where you got `RandomSplitter`:

```
from __future__ import absolute_import

from packtml.decision_tree.cart import RandomSplitter
from packtml.decision_tree.metrics import InformationGain
import numpy as np
```

We already looked at `InformationGain` a little bit in the last section to compute our information gain candidate split. Here, we will look at how we actually create the candidate split. We get the following data along with the corresponding class labels:

```
# Build the example from the slides (3.3)
X = np.array([[21, 3], [ 4, 2], [37, 2]])
y = np.array([1, 0, 1])
```

RandomSplitter will evaluate each of the preceding values since n_val_sample is 3. So, it's going to compute three candidates split points for each feature, and we will find out which of them are the best:

```
# this is the splitting class; we'll use gini as the criteria
random_state = np.random.RandomState(42)
splitter = RandomSplitter(random_state=random_state,
                          criterion=InformationGain('gini'),
                          n_val_sample=3)
# find the best:
best_feature, best_value, best_gain = splitter.find_best(X, y)
print("Best feature=%i, best value=%r, information gain: %.3f"
      % (best_feature, best_value, best_gain))
```

When we run the preceding code, we see best_feature is 0 and best_value is 21, meaning that anything greater than or equal to 21 in feature 0 will go left, and everything else goes right. The InformationGain we get is 0.444, which, sure enough, when we computed it by hand, is exactly what we expected:

```
(packt-sml) test@test-Veriton-Series:~/Documents/Hands-on-Supervised-Machine-Learning-with-Python-master/examples/decision_tree$ pyth
on example_classification_split.py
Best feature=0, best value=21, information gain: 0.444
```

In the next section, we'll cover how we can implement a decision tree from scratch inside the packtml library.

Implementing a decision tree from scratch

We will start out by looking at the implementation of our splitting metrics. Then we'll cover some of our splitting logic, and finally, we'll see how we can wrap the tree so that we can generalize from classification and regression tasks.

Classification tree

Let's go ahead and walk through a classification tree example. We will be using the information gain criteria. In PyCharm there are three scripts open, two of which are metrics.py and cart.py, both of which are found inside of the packtml/decision_tree submodule. Then we have the example_classification_decision_tree.py file, which is in examples/decision_tree. Let's start with metrics.

If you open up the `cart.py` file, we have an order in which we should step through this so that you can understand how the decision tree class is going to work:

```
# 1. metrics.InformationGain & metrics.VarianceReduction
# 2. RandomSplitter
# 3. LeafNode
# 4. BaseCART
```

Starting with the `metrics.py` file from the top, you can see that _all_ is going to include four different metrics:

```
__all__ = [
    'entropy',
    'gini_impurity',
    'InformationGain',
    'VarianceReduction'
]
```

`entropy` and `gini_impurity` are both classification metrics. We have talked about `gini_impurity`. You can see here that both of them are calling the `clf_metric` private function as shown:

```
def entropy(y):
    """Compute the entropy of class labels.

    This computes the entropy of training samples. A high entropy means
    a relatively uniform distribution, while low entropy indicates a
    varying distribution (many peaks and valleys).

    References
    ----------
    .. [1]
http://www.cs.csi.cuny.edu/~imberman/ai/Entropy%20and%20Information%20Gain.
htm
    """
    return _clf_metric(y, 'entropy')


def gini_impurity(y):
    """Compute the Gini index on a target variable.

    The Gini index gives an idea of how mixed two classes are within a leaf
    node. A perfect class separation will result in a Gini impurity of 0
(that is,
    "perfectly pure").
    """
    return _clf_metric(y, 'gini')
```

Now, `gini` and `entropy` acts essentially the same way, except that at the end, `gini` computes a norm essentially on itself where `entropy` is `log2`:

```
def _clf_metric(y, metric):
    """Internal helper. Since this is internal, so no validation
performed"""
    # get unique classes in y
    y = np.asarray(y)
    C, cts = np.unique(y, return_counts=True)

    # a base case is that there is only one class label
    if C.shape[0] == 1:
        return 0.

    pr_C = cts.astype(float) / y.shape[0] # P(Ci)

    # 1 - sum(P(Ci)^2)
    if metric == 'gini':
        return 1. - pr_C.dot(pr_C) # np.sum(pr_C ** 2)
    elif metric == 'entropy':
        return np.sum(-pr_C * np.log2(pr_C))

    # shouldn't ever get to this point since it is internal
    else:
        raise ValueError("metric should be one of ('gini', 'entropy'), "
                         "but encountered %s" % metric)
```

One thing to note here is that entropy and Gini are going to make a huge difference in how your tree performs. Gini is actually canon for the CART algorithm, but we included entropy here so you could see that this is something you can use if you want to.

`BaseCriterion` is our base class for a splitting criterion. We have two splitting criteria, `InformationGain` and `VarianceReduction`. Both of them are going to implement `compute_uncertainty`:

```
class BaseCriterion(object):
    """Splitting criterion.

    Base class for InformationGain and VarianceReduction. WARNING - do
    not invoke this class directly. Use derived classes only! This is a
    loosely-defined abstract class used to prescribe a common interface
    for sub-classes.
    """
    def compute_uncertainty(self, y):
        """Compute the uncertainty for a vector.
```

```
            A subclass should override this function to compute the uncertainty
            (that is, entropy or gini) of a vector.
            """


    class InformationGain(BaseCriterion):
        """Compute the information gain after a split.

        The information gain metric is used by CART trees in a classification
        context. It measures the difference in the gini or entropy before and
        after a split to determine whether the split "taught" us anything.
```

If you remember from the last section, uncertainty is essentially the level of impurity, or entropy, induced by the split. When we compute InformationGain using either gini or entropy, our uncertainty is going to be metric pre-split:

```
    def __init__(self, metric):
            # let fail out with a KeyError if an improper metric
            self.crit = {'gini': gini_impurity,
                         'entropy': entropy}[metric]
```

If we compute uncertainty, we would pass in a node and say compute Gini, for instance, on all of the samples inside of the node before we split, and then, when we call to actually compute InformationGain, we pass in mask for whether something is going left or right. We will compute the Gini on the left and right side, and return InformationGain:

```
    def __call__(self, target, mask, uncertainty):
            """Compute the information gain of a split.

            Parameters
            ----------
            target : np.ndarray
                The target feature

            mask : np.ndarray
                The value mask

            uncertainty : float
                The gini or entropy of rows pre-split
            """
            left, right = target[mask], target[~mask]
            p = float(left.shape[0]) / float(target.shape[0])

            crit = self.crit # type: callable
            return uncertainty - p * crit(left) - (1 - p) * crit(right)
```

This is how we compute `InformationGain`, and this is just the wrapper class that we have built. `VarianceReduction` is very similar, except the `compute_uncertainty` function is simply going to return the variance of *y*. When we call this, we are subtracting the uncertainty of the pre-split node, minus the sum of the uncertainties for the left and right on the split. What we're doing here is maximizing the reduction of the variance between each split respectively. That way, we can know if a split is good. It separates along a relatively intuitive line, as follows:

```
class VarianceReduction(BaseCriterion):
    """Compute the variance reduction after a split.

    Variance reduction is a splitting criterion used by CART trees in the
    context of regression. It examines the variance in a target before and
    after a split to determine whether we've reduced the variability in the
    target.
    """
    def compute_uncertainty(self, y):
        """Compute the variance of a target."""
        return np.var(y)

    def __call__(self, target, mask, uncertainty):
        left, right = target[mask], target[~mask]
        return uncertainty - (self.compute_uncertainty(left) +
                              self.compute_uncertainty(right))
```

These are our two splitting criteria: `InformationGain` and `VarianceReduction`. We're going to use `InformationGain` for classification and `VarianceReduction` for regression. Since we're talking about classification right now, let's focus on `InformationGain`. Moving over to the `cart.py` file, we see that the next thing we want to talk about is `RandomSplitter`.

In one of the last sections, we learned about a strategy to produce candidate splits. This is essentially `RandomSplitter`. There are a lot of different strategies you can use here. We're going to use a bit of entropy so that we can get through this class and this algorithm relatively quickly, without getting into the nitty-gritty.

`RandomSplitter` will take several arguments. We want `random_state` so that we can replicate this split later. The criterion is an instance of either `InformationGain` or `VarianceReduction` and the number of values that we want to sample from each feature:

```
def __init__(self, random_state, criterion, n_val_sample=25):
        self.random_state = random_state
        self.criterion = criterion # BaseCriterion from metrics
        self.n_val_sample = n_val_sample
```

So, our `find_best` function will scan the entire feature space, sample the number of values per split or per feature, and determine `best_value` and `best_feature` on which to split. This will produce our best split for the tree at the time. So, `best_gain` will start as 0. If it's negative it's a bad one, so we don't want to split at all. If it's positive then it's better than our current best, and so we'll take that and increment it to find our best. We want to find our `best_feature` and our `best_value`:

```
def find_best(self, X, y):
        criterion = self.criterion
        rs = self.random_state

        # keep track of the best info gain
        best_gain = 0.

        # keep track of best feature and best value on which to split
        best_feature = None
        best_value = None

        # get the current state of the uncertainty (gini or entropy)
        uncertainty = criterion.compute_uncertainty(y)
```

Now, for each of the columns of our dataset, we're going to go ahead and grab out the feature. This is just a NumPy array, a 1D NumPy array:

```
# iterate over each feature
for col in xrange(X.shape[1]):
    feature = X[:, col]
```

We will create a set so that we can keep track of which values we have already seen, if we happen to sample the same one over and over again. We will permute this feature so that we can shuffle it up and scan over each of the values in the feature. One thing you'll note here is that we could collect just the unique values of the feature. But first of all, it's kind of expensive to get the unique values. Secondly, that throws away all the distributional information about the feature. By doing this, we happen to have more of a certain value than another, or more values grouped more closely together. This is going to allow us to get a little bit more of a true sample of the feature itself:

```
# For each of n_val_sample iterations, select a random value
# from the feature and create a split. We store whether we've seen
# the value before; if we have, continue. Continue until we've seen
# n_vals unique values. This allows us to more likely select values
# that are high frequency (retains distributional data implicitly)
for v in rs.permutation(feature):
```

If the number of `seen_values` in our set is equal to the number of values that we want to sample, we're going to break out. So, if we say there are `100` unique values, but we've already seen `25`, we're going to break out. Otherwise, if we have already seen this value in that set, we're going to keep going. We don't want to compute the same thing over a value that we have already computed. So, here we will add that value to the set, and create our mask for whether we split left or right:

```
# if we've hit the limit of the number of values we wanted to
# examine, break out
if len(seen_values) == n_vals:
    break
# if we've already tried this value, continue
elif v in seen_values: # O(1) lookup
    continue
# otherwise, it's a new value we've never tried splitting on.
# add it to the set.
seen_values.add(v)

# create the mask (these values "go left")
mask = feature >= v # type: np.ndarray
```

Now, there's one more corner case. If we have grabbed the minimum value, then our mask is going to take everything in one direction, which is what this is checking. We don't want that, because, otherwise, we're not creating a true split. So, if that's the case, then we `continue`, and sample again:

```
# skip this step if this doesn't divide the dataset
if np.unique(mask).shape[0] == 1: # all True or all False
    continue
```

Now let's compute the gain, either `InformationGain` or `VarianceReduction`, which computes the Gini on the left and right side and subtracts that from the original uncertainty. If the `gain` is good, meaning if it's better than the current best we've seen, then we have a new `best_feature` and a new `best_value`, and we store that. So, we loop over this and go over the randomly sampled values within each feature and determine the `best_feature` to split on and the `best_value` in that feature to split on. If we don't have one, it means we never found a viable split, which happens in rare cases:

```
# compute how good this split was
gain = criterion(y, mask, uncertainty=uncertainty)

# if the gain is better, we keep this feature & value &
# update the best gain we've seen so far
if gain > best_gain:
    best_feature = col
    best_value = v
```

```
        best_gain = gain

    # if best feature is None, it means we never found a viable split...
    # this is likely because all of our labels were perfect. In this case,
    # we could select any feature and the first value and define that as
    # our left split and nothing will go right.
    if best_feature is None:
        best_feature = 0
        best_value = np.squeeze(X[:, best_feature])[0]
        best_gain = 0.

    # we need to know the best feature, the best value, and the best gain
    return best_feature, best_value, best_gain
```

Next, we will look in `LeafNode`. If you have ever built a binary tree before, then you would be familiar with the concept of `LeafNode`. `LeafNode` is going to store a left and a right pointer, both typically initialized to null to show that there's nothing there. So, the leaf node, in this case, is going to be the guts of our decision tree. It provides the skeleton where the tree itself is just a wrapper:

```
class LeafNode(object):
    """A tree node class.

    Tree node that store the column on which to split and the value above
    which to go left vs. right. Additionally, it stores the target
statistic
    related to this node. For instance, in a classification scenario:

        >>> X = np.array([[ 1, 1.5 ],
        ...               [ 2, 0.5 ],
        ...               [ 3, 0.75]])
        >>> y = np.array([0, 1, 1])
        >>> node = LeafNode(split_col=0, split_val=2,
        ...             class_statistic=_most_common(y))
```

`LeafNode` is going to store `split_col`, the feature that we are splitting on, `split_val`, and `split_gain`, as well as `class_statistic`. So, `class_statistic` for classification is going to be the node, where we vote for the most common value. In regression, it's going to be the mean. If you want to get really fancy you might use the median or some other strategy for regression. However, we're just going to use the mean because we're keeping it simple here. So, a constructor is going to store these values and initialize our left and right as null again:

```
    def __init__(self, split_col, split_val, split_gain, class_statistic):

        self.split_col = split_col
```

```
        self.split_val = split_val
        self.split_gain = split_gain

        # the class statistic is the mode or the mean of the targets for
        # this split
        self.class_statistic = class_statistic

        # if these remain None, it's a terminal node
        self.left = None
        self.right = None

    def create_split(self, X, y):
        """Split the next X, y.
```

Now in the `create_split` function, we actually get to the tree structure itself. But this is going to essentially split the node and create a new left and right. Hence, it goes from the terminal node to the next split downward, which we can recurse over. We will take the current set for that current dataset from the X and y split. Given that the value in the feature that we have already initialized will create our mask for left and right, if we're going all left or all right, that's where it stores. Otherwise, it's going to produce this split, segmenting out the rows on the left side and the rows on the right side, or else the rows are none. If there's no split on the left/right, we just use none and we will return X_left, X_right, y_left and y_right:

```
# If values in the split column are greater than or equal to the
# split value, we go left.
left_mask = X[:, self.split_col] >= self.split_val

# Otherwise we go to the right
right_mask = ~left_mask # type: np.ndarray

# If the left mask is all False or all True, it means we've achieved
# a perfect split.
all_left = left_mask.all()
all_right = right_mask.all()

# create the left split. If it's all right side, we'll return None
X_left = X[left_mask, :] if not all_right else None
y_left = y[left_mask] if not all_right else None

# create the right split. If it's all left side, we'll return None.
X_right = X[right_mask, :] if not all_left else None
y_right = y[right_mask] if not all_left else None

return X_left, X_right, y_left, y_right
```

The terminal is just a shortcut here for left and right. If we have either, then it's not terminal. But, if it has both null for left and right, then it's a terminal node:

```
def is_terminal(self):
    """Determine whether the node is terminal.

    If there is no left node and no right node, it's a terminal node.
    If either is non-None, it is a parent to something.
    """
    return self.left is None and self.right is None
```

We will use the `predict_record` function internally for producing predictions inside LeafNode. This is going to use that `class_statistic` function that we have. `class_statistic` is either the mode for classification or the mean for regression. For predicting whether or not a record goes left or right, we recurse down, and that is just what is happening here in `predict`, which we'll get to, and look at how we produce predictions:

```
def predict_record(self, record):
    """Find the terminal node in the tree and return the class
statistic"""
        # First base case, this is a terminal node:
        has_left = self.left is not None
        has_right = self.right is not None
        if not has_left and not has_right:
            return self.class_statistic

        # Otherwise, determine whether the record goes right or left
        go_left = record[self.split_col] >= self.split_val

        # if we go left and there is a left node, delegate the recursion to
the
        # left side
        if go_left and has_left:
            return self.left.predict_record(record)

        # if we go right, delegate to the right
        if not go_left and has_right:
            return self.right.predict_record(record)

        # if we get here, it means one of two things:
        # 1. we were supposed to go left and didn't have a left
        # 2. we were supposed to go right and didn't have a right
        # for both of these, we return THIS class statistic
        return self.class_statistic
```

Now, the trees themselves are two classes. We have CARTRegressor and CARTClassifier. Both of these are going to wrap the BaseCART class, which we will walk through right now. BaseCART, as with most of our base simple estimators that we've already walked through, is going to take two arguments for certain, which are X and y—our training data and our training labels. It's also going to take our criterion, which we will pass at the bottom. It's either your InformationGain for classification, VarianceReduction for regression, min_samples_split, and all these other hyperparameters, which we've already kind of talked through. The first thing we're going to do is, as usual, check our X and y to make sure that we have all continuous values, that we're not missing any data. This is just assigning self attributes for the hyperparameters and we will create our splitter as RandomSplitter, which we're going to use in this process. This is how we grow the tree. It all happens in find_next_split. So, this is going to take three arguments. We've got our X, our y, and then the count:

```python
class _BaseCART(BaseSimpleEstimator):
    def __init__(self, X, y, criterion, min_samples_split, max_depth,
                 n_val_sample, random_state):
        # make sure max_depth > 1
        if max_depth < 2:
            raise ValueError("max depth must be > 1")

        # check the input arrays, and if it's classification validate the
        # target values in y
        X, y = check_X_y(X, y, accept_sparse=False, dtype=None, copy=True)
        if is_classifier(self):
            check_classification_targets(y)

        # hyper parameters so we can later inspect attributes of the model
        self.min_samples_split = min_samples_split
        self.max_depth = max_depth
        self.n_val_sample = n_val_sample
        self.random_state = random_state

        # create the splitting class
        random_state = check_random_state(random_state)
        self.splitter = RandomSplitter(random_state, criterion,
n_val_sample)

        # grow the tree depth first
        self.tree = self._find_next_split(X, y, 0)
```

Essentially, we will recurse over the `find_next_split` function until our tree is fully grown or pruned. Since we're recursing, we always set our base case first. If `current_depth` is equal to `maximum_depth` that we want to grow a tree, or the size, the number of samples in X, is less than or equal to the `min_samples_split` in our split, both of which are our terminal criteria, and we will return `None`:

```
def _find_next_split(self, X, y, current_depth):
    # base case 1: current depth is the limit, the parent node should
    # be a terminal node (child = None)
    # base case 2: n samples in X <= min_samples_split
    if current_depth == self.max_depth or \
            X.shape[0] <= self.min_samples_split:
        return None
```

Otherwise, we will grab our splitter and find the best split between X and y, which gives us our `best_feature`, `best_value`, and `gain`, either `VarianceReduction` or `InformationGain`. Next, we have just found our first split. So, now we will create the node that corresponds to that split. The node is going to take all of those same arguments, plus the target statistics. When we produce predictions for the node, if it's terminal, we return the node for that label; otherwise, we return the mean for our training labels. That's how we assign that prediction there. So, now we have our node, and we want to create our split. So, we get `X_right` and `X_left`. We can recurse down both sides of the tree. We will use that node to create the split on X and Y. So, if X is `None`, `X_left` is `None`, which means we're not going to go down to the left side anymore. If it is not `None`, then we can assign a node to the left, which is going to recurse on `find_next_split`. If `X_right` is `None` then it means we're not going to grow it on the right anymore. If it's not `None`, we can do the same thing. So, we're going to assign our right side by recursing down `find_next_split`. We recurse over this, continually adding `current_depth + 1`, until one side has reached its `maximum_depth`. Otherwise, the size of the splits are no longer long enough for `min_sample_split` and we stop growing. So, we reach that point where we stop growing:

```
# create the next split
split_feature, split_value, gain = \
    self.splitter.find_best(X, y)

# create the next node based on the best split feature and value
# that we just found. Also compute the "target stat" (mode of y for
# classification problems or mean of y for regression problems) and
# pass that to the node in case it is the terminal node (that is, the
# decision maker)
node = LeafNode(split_feature, split_value, gain, self._target_stat(y))
# Create the splits based on the criteria we just determined, and then
# recurse down left, right sides
X_left, X_right, y_left, y_right = node.create_split(X, y)
```

```
# if either the left or right is None, it means we've achieved a
# perfect split. It is then a terminal node and will remain None.
if X_left is not None:
    node.left = self._find_next_split(X_left, y_left,
                                      current_depth + 1)
```

Now, for predicting, we will traverse down the tree until we find the point where a record belongs. So, for each row in X, we will predict a row, which we have already looked at in the LeafNode class, traversing down the left or right until we find the node where that row belongs. Then we'll return class_statistics. So, if the row gets to a node, it says this belongs here. If the node for that class, for classification, was 1, then we return 1. Otherwise, if the mean was, say, 5.6, then we return the same. That's how we produce these predictions, which we're just going to bundle into a NumPy array:

```
def predict(self, X):
    # Check the array
    X = check_array(X, dtype=np.float32) # type: np.ndarray

    # For each record in X, find its leaf node in the tree (O(log N))
    # to get the predictions. This makes the prediction operation
    # O(N log N) runtime complexity
    predictions = [self.tree.predict_record(row) for row in X]
    return np.asarray(predictions)
```

So, let's look at how a classification decision tree can perform on some real data. In the following example script, we will import CARTClassifier:

```
from packtml.decision_tree import CARTClassifier
from packtml.utils.plotting import add_decision_boundary_to_axis
from sklearn.metrics import accuracy_score
from sklearn.model_selection import train_test_split
import matplotlib.pyplot as plt
import numpy as np
import sys
```

We will create two different bubbles inside of our 2D access on multivariate_normal. Using this multivariate_normal inside of RandomState, we will stack that all together and produce train_test_split as usual:

```
# Create a classification dataset
rs = np.random.RandomState(42)
covariance = [[1, .75], [.75, 1]]
n_obs = 500
x1 = rs.multivariate_normal(mean=[0, 0], cov=covariance, size=n_obs)
x2 = rs.multivariate_normal(mean=[1, 3], cov=covariance, size=n_obs)
```

```
X = np.vstack((x1, x2)).astype(np.float32)
y = np.hstack((np.zeros(n_obs), np.ones(n_obs)))

# split the data
X_train, X_test, y_train, y_test = train_test_split(X, y, random_state=42)
```

We will fit `CARTClassifier` and perform two different classifiers. We will do the first one. Knowing what you now know about variance and bias, you know that classifier or non-parametric models, particularly the decision tree, are capable of having very high variance: they can overfit really easily. So, if we use a really shallow depth, then we're more likely to not overfit. In the second one, we're going to try to overfit as much as we can with a max depth of 25. Since we have a pretty small dataset, we can be reasonably certain that this is probably going to overfit. We'll see that when we look at the actual output of this example:

```
# Fit a simple decision tree classifier and get predictions
shallow_depth = 2
clf = CARTClassifier(X_train, y_train, max_depth=shallow_depth,
criterion='gini',
                    random_state=42)
pred = clf.predict(X_test)
clf_accuracy = accuracy_score(y_test, pred)
print("Test accuracy (depth=%i): %.3f" % (shallow_depth, clf_accuracy))

# Fit a deeper tree and show accuracy increases
clf2 = CARTClassifier(X_train, y_train, max_depth=25, criterion='gini',
                    random_state=42)
pred2 = clf2.predict(X_test)
clf2_accuracy = accuracy_score(y_test, pred2)
print("Test accuracy (depth=25): %.3f" % clf2_accuracy)
```

So, we fit the two of these, look at the accuracy, and plot them. Let's go ahead and run the code and see how it looks:

```
(packt-sml) test@test-Veriton-Series:~/Documents/Hands-on-Supervised-Machine-Learning-with-Python-master$ python examples/decision_tr
ee/example_classification_decision_tree.py
Test accuracy (depth=2): 0.952
Test accuracy (depth=25): 0.972
```

If you run the preceding code, we get the test's accuracy of 95% on our underfitted tree as shown:

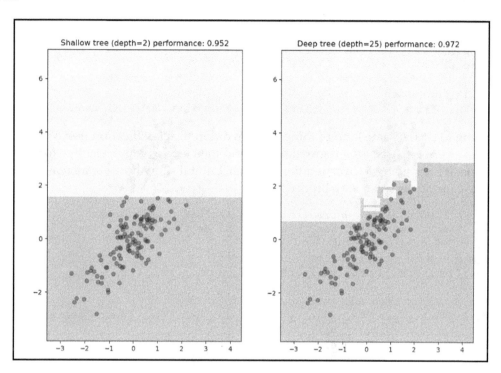

Regression tree

Now let's see how a regression tree can perform. We walked through the same exact implementation of our regression tree, except we're going to use the variance reduction. Rather than using the mode voting here for producing predictions, we're going to use the mean.

Inside the `examples` directory, we have the `example_regression_decision_tree.py` file. So, here we will import `CARTRegressor` and use `mean_squared_error` as our loss function to determine how well we did:

```
from packtml.decision_tree import CARTRegressor
from sklearn.metrics import mean_squared_error
from sklearn.model_selection import train_test_split
import matplotlib.pyplot as plt
import numpy as np
import sys
```

We will just create random values here in a sine wave. That's what we want to be our function as our output here:

```
# Create a classification dataset
rs = np.random.RandomState(42)
X = np.sort(5 * rs.rand(80, 1), axis=0)
y = np.sin(X).ravel()

# split the data
X_train, X_test, y_train, y_test = train_test_split(X, y, random_state=42)
```

We're going to do the same kind of thing that we did in the classification tree. We will fit a simple `max_depth=3` tree for a regression tree and then a `max_depth=10` tree for the second one. It's not going to overfit quite as much, but it'll show how we increase our predictive capacity as we grow a bit deeper:

```
# Fit a simple decision tree regressor and get predictions
clf = CARTRegressor(X_train, y_train, max_depth=3, random_state=42)
pred = clf.predict(X_test)
clf_mse = mean_squared_error(y_test, pred)
print("Test MSE (depth=3): %.3f" % clf_mse)

# Fit a deeper tree and show accuracy increases
clf2 = CARTRegressor(X_train, y_train, max_depth=10, random_state=42)
pred2 = clf2.predict(X_test)
clf2_mse = mean_squared_error(y_test, pred2)
print("Test MSE (depth=10): %.3f" % clf2_mse)
```

Here, we're just plotting the outputs:

```
x = X_train.ravel()
xte = X_test.ravel()

fig, axes = plt.subplots(1, 2, figsize=(12, 8))
axes[0].scatter(x, y_train, alpha=0.25, c='r')
axes[0].scatter(xte, pred, alpha=1.)
axes[0].set_title("Shallow tree (depth=3) test MSE: %.3f" % clf_mse)

axes[1].scatter(x, y_train, alpha=0.4, c='r')
axes[1].scatter(xte, pred2, alpha=1.)
axes[1].set_title("Deeper tree (depth=10) test MSE: %.3f" % clf2_mse)

# if we're supposed to save it, do so INSTEAD OF showing it
if len(sys.argv) > 1:
    plt.savefig(sys.argv[1])
else:
    plt.show()
```

Let's go ahead and run this. Rather than `example_classification_decision_tree.py`, we're going to run `example_regression_decision_tree.py`:

```
(packt-sml) test@test-Veriton-Series:~/Documents/Hands-on-Supervised-Machine-Learning-with-Python-master$ python examples/decision_tr
ee/example_regression_decision_tree.py
Test MSE (depth=3): 0.084
Test MSE (depth=10): 0.005
```

So, first, you can see that our mean squared error decreases with the `max_depth` growing, which is good. You can also see that our outcome starts to model this sine wave pretty well as we increase the depth, and we're able to learn this non-linear function very well:

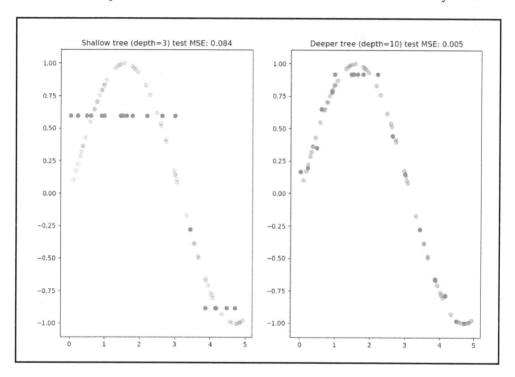

In the next section, we're going to look at clustering methods and move on from decision trees.

Various clustering methods

In this section, we will cover the different clustering methods. First, let's look at what clustering is. Then we'll explain some of the mathematical tricks that we can use in clustering. And finally, we're going to introduce our newest non-parametric algorithm KNN.

What is clustering?

Clustering is about as intuitive as it gets in terms of machine learning models. The idea is we can segment groups of samples based on their nearness to one another. The hypothesis is the samples that are closer are more similar in some respects. So, there are two reasons we might want to cluster. The first is for discovery purposes, and we usually do this when we make no assumptions about the underlying structure of the data, or don't have labels. And so, this typically is done in a purely unsupervised sense. But as this is obviously a supervised learning book, we're going to focus on the second use case, which uses clustering as a classification technique.

Distance metrics

So, before we get into the algorithms, I want to address some mathematical esotericism. When you have two points, or any number of points, in a 2D space, it's fairly easy to conceptualize. It's basically calculating the hypotenuse along some right triangle, in terms of measuring the distance. However, what happens when you have a really high dimensional space? That's what we're going to get into, and we have a lot of clustering problems.

So, the most common distance metric is the Euclidean distance. This is essentially a generalization of the 2D approach. It's the square root of the sum of squared differences between two vectors, and it can be used in any dimensional space. There's a lot of others that we're not going to get into. Two of them are **Manhattan** and **Mahalanobis**. Manhattan is a lot like the Euclidean distance. However, rather than having the squared difference, it's going to have the absolute value of the difference.

KNN – introduction

KNN is a really simple intuitive approach to building a clustering classifier. The idea is, given a set of labeled samples, when a new sample is introduced, we look at the k nearest points, and we make an estimate for its class membership based on the majority of points around it. So, in the following diagram we would classify this new question mark as a positive sample since the majority of its neighbors are positive:

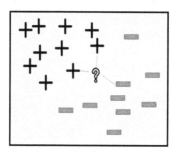

KNN – considerations

There are a few considerations you should take into account here. KNN is a bit interesting and can fluctuate between wildly high bias or high variance depending on its hyperparameter K. If K is too large and you're comparing a new sample to the entire training set, it favors the majority class. Essentially, whichever is more, we vote that way. This would be a highly underfitted model. If K is too small, it gives higher priority to the immediately adjacent samples, which means that the model is extremely overfitted. In addition to considerations around K, you may also want to consider centering and scaling your data. Otherwise, your distance metric will not be very sensitive to small-scale features. For instance, if one of your features is thousands of dollars for a house and the other feature is the number of bathrooms, *1.5* to *3.5* or so, you're going to implicitly be favoring the dollars versus the number of bathrooms. So, you might want to center and scale.

A classic KNN algorithm

A classic KNN algorithm will compute the distances between the training samples and store them in a distance-partitioned heap structure, such as **KDTree** or a ball tree, which are essentially sorted-heap binary trees. We then query the tree for test samples. Our approach in this class is going to be a little bit different in order to be a bit more intuitive and readable.

In the next section, we'll cover how we can implement it from scratch.

Implementing KNNs from scratch

In this section, we will jump into the `packtml` code base, and see how we can implement it from scratch. We'll start by revisiting the classic algorithm we covered in the last section, and then we'll look at the actual Python code, which has some implementation changes.

Recall the archetypal KNN algorithm. The efficient implementation is going to be to pre-compute the distances and store them in a special heap. Of course, with most things in computer science, there's the clever way and then there's the easy-to-read way. We're going to do things a bit differently in an effort to maximize the readability, but it's the same fundamental algorithm.

KNN clustering

We've got two files we want to look at. The first is the source code in the `packtml` Python package. Second, we're going to look an example of the KNN applied to the `iris` dataset. Let's go ahead and jump over to PyCharm, where there are two files open. Inside of the `clustering` submodule, we have the `knn.py` file open. This is where we're going to find the KNN class and all the implementation details. Then in the examples directory, in the `clustering` subdirectory, we have the `example_knn_classifier.py` file open as well. We'll walk through that after we've gone through the implementation details.

Now, regarding other libraries, we're going to use scikit-learn's utils to validate the X, y, and classification targets. However, we're also going to use the `metrics.pairwise` submodule to use `euclidean_distances`:

```
from __future__ import absolute_import

from sklearn.metrics.pairwise import euclidean_distances
from sklearn.utils.validation import check_X_y
from sklearn.utils.multiclass import check_classification_targets
```

If we want to use a different distance metric, we could also import Manhattan, as mentioned in the earlier section. But for this, we're just going to use Euclidean. So, if you want to adjust that later, feel free. Our KNN class here is going to take three parameters. As usual for `BaseSimpleEstimator`, we're going to take our X and y, which are our training vectors and our training label, and then k, which is our tuning parameter for the number of neighbors that we want to compute around each sample:

```
Parameters
----------
X : array-like, shape=(n_samples, n_features)
```

The training array. Should be a numpy array or array-like structure
with only finite values.

```
y : array-like, shape=(n_samples,)
    The target vector.
k : int, optional (default=10)
    The number of neighbors to identify. The higher the ``k`` parameter,
    the more likely you are to *under*-fit your data. The lower the ``k``
    parameter, the more likely you are to *over*-fit your model.
```

So, our constructor is pretty simple. We're going to check our X and y and basically store them. Then we assign k to a `self` attribute. Now, in other implementations we might go ahead and compute our KDTree or our ball tree:

```python
def __init__(self, X, y, k=10):
    # check the input array
    X, y = check_X_y(X, y, accept_sparse=False, dtype=np.float32,
                     copy=True)

    # make sure we're performing classification here
    check_classification_targets(y)

    # Save the K hyper-parameter so we can use it later
    self.k = k

    # kNN is a special case where we have to save the training data in
    # order to make predictions in the future
    self.X = X
    self.y = y
```

So, we're going to do a brute force method, where we don't compute the distances until we predict. This is a lazy evaluation of distances. In our predict function, we are going to take our X, which is our test array. X, which we assigned in the constructor. We will compute `euclidean_distances` between our training array and our test array. Here, we get an M by M matrix, where M is the number of samples in our test array:

```python
def predict(self, X):
    # Compute the pairwise distances between each observation in
    # the dataset and the training data. This can be relatively expensive
    # for very large datasets!!
    train = self.X
    dists = euclidean_distances(X, train)
```

In order to find the nearest distance, we `argsort` distances by the column to show which samples are closest. Following, is the array of distances, and we are going to `argsort` it along the `axis` column, such that we get the samples that are closest, based on the distance:

```
# Arg sort to find the shortest distance for each row. This sorts
# elements in each row (independent of other rows) to determine the
# order required to sort the rows.
# that is:
# >>> P = np.array([[4, 5, 1], [3, 1, 6]])
# >>> np.argsort(P, axis=1)
# array([[2, 0, 1],
# [1, 0, 2]])
nearest = np.argsort(dists, axis=1)
```

We will slice the labels based on `top_k` along y. These are basically the class labels:

```
# We only care about the top K, really, so get sorted and then truncate
# that is:
# array([[1, 2, 1],
# ...
# [0, 0, 0]])
predicted_labels = self.y[nearest][:, :self.k]
```

Since it's a classification, we're interested in `mode`. Take the mode using the `mode` function along that `axis` and `ravel` it into a NumPy array:

```
# We want the most common along the rows as the predictions
# that is:
# array([1, ..., 0])
return mode(predicted_labels, axis=1)[0].ravel()
```

Hence, we're just computing the distances for the predict function, argsorting the closest distances, then finding the corresponding labels, and taking the mode. Now, over in the `examples/clustering` directory, go to `example_knn_classifier.py`. We're going to use the `load_iris` function from scikit-learn:

```
from __future__ import absolute_import

from packtml.clustering import KNNClassifier
from packtml.utils.plotting import add_decision_boundary_to_axis
from sklearn.model_selection import train_test_split
from sklearn.preprocessing import StandardScaler
from sklearn.metrics import accuracy_score
from sklearn.datasets import load_iris
from matplotlib import pyplot as plt
from matplotlib.colors import ListedColormap
import sys
```

We will only use the first two dimensions so that we can visualize it in a relatively intuitive fashion. Perform the training split, and then center and scale using `StandardScaler`:

```
# Create a classification sub-dataset using iris
iris = load_iris()
X = iris.data[:, :2] # just use the first two dimensions
y = iris.target

# split data
X_train, X_test, y_train, y_test = train_test_split(X, y, random_state=42)

# scale the data
scaler = StandardScaler()
X_train = scaler.fit_transform(X_train)
X_test = scaler.transform(X_test)
```

Fit the `KNNClassifier` with k=10:

```
# Fit a k-nearest neighbor model and get predictions
k=10
clf = KNNClassifier(X_train, y_train, k=k)
pred = clf.predict(X_test)
clf_accuracy = accuracy_score(y_test, pred)
print("Test accuracy: %.3f" % clf_accuracy)
```

Finally, we will plot it by typing the following command. Make sure you've got your environment activated, as usual:

```
(packt-sml) test@test-Veriton-Series:~/Downloads/Hands-on-Supervised-Machine-Learning-with-Python-master/examples/clustering$ python
example_knn_classifier.py
Test accuracy: 0.711
```

The output for k = 10, and we get about 73-74% test accuracy. Note that we're only using two dimensions:

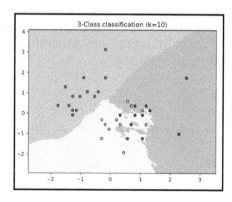

So, now that you're a KNN expert, you can build one from scratch. In the next section, we will compare non-parametric models to parametric models.

Non-parametric models – pros/cons

In this section, we will discuss every statistician's favorite philosophical debate, which is the pros and cons of non-parametric models versus parametric models.

Pros of non-parametric models

Non-parametric models are able to learn some really complex relationships between your predictors and the output variable, which can make them really powerful for non-trivial modeling problems. Just like the regression sinusoidal wave we modeled in the decision trees, a lot of non-parametric models are fairly tolerant to data scale as well. The major exception here is the clustering techniques, but these techniques can pose a major advantage for models such as decision trees, which don't require the same level of pre-processing that parametric models might. Finally, if you find yourself suffering from high variance, you can always add more training data, with which your model is likely to get better.

Cons of non-parametric models

There are the not-so-good parts of non-parametric models as well. Several of these we have already covered. So, as you may know, they can be slower to fit or predict, and less intuitive in many cases than a lot of parametric models. If speed is less critical than accuracy, non-parametric models may be a great candidate for your model. Likewise, with explainability, these models can be over-complicated and tough to understand. Finally, one of the advantages of non-parametric models is the ability to get better with more data, which can be a weakness if data is hard to get. They generally do require a bit more data to train effectively than their parametric brethren.

Which model to use?

Parametric models that we've already covered have some really great and convenient attributes. There are several reasons you may opt for a parametric model over a non-parametric model. Particularly if you're in a regulated industry, we need to explain the models more easily. Non-parametric models, on the other hand, may create a better, more complex model. But if you don't have a good chunk of data, it may not perform very well. It is best not to get overly philosophical about which one you should or should not use. Just use whichever best fits your data and meets your business requirements.

Summary

In this chapter, we initially got introduced to non-parametric models and then we walked through the decision trees. In the next sections, we learned the splitting criteria and how they produce splits. We also learned about the bias-variance trade-off, and how non-parametric models tend to favor a higher variance set of error, while parametric models favor high bias. Next, we looked into clustering methods and even coded a KNN class from scratch. Finally, we wrapped up with the pros and cons of non-parametric methods.

In the next chapter, we will get into some more of the advanced topics in supervised machine learning, including recommender systems and neural networks.

4
Advanced Topics in Supervised Machine Learning

In this chapter, we're going to focus on some advanced topics. We'll cover two topics: recommender systems and neural networks. We'll start with collaborative filtering, and then we'll look at integrating content-based similarities into collaborative filtering systems. We'll get into neural networks and transfer learning. Finally, we'll introduce the math and concept behind each of these, before getting into Python code.

We will cover the following topics:

- Recommended systems and an introduction to collaborative filtering
- Matrix factorization
- Content-based filtering
- Neural networks and deep learning
- Using transfer learning

Technical requirements

For this chapter, you will need to install the following software, if you haven't already done so:

- Jupyter Notebook
- Anaconda
- Python

The code files for this chapter can be found at `https://github.com/PacktPublishing/Supervised-Machine-Learning-with-Python`.

Recommended systems and an introduction to collaborative filtering

In this section, we'll cover collaborative filtering and recommender systems. We'll start out by explaining what may constitute a recommender system, how users willingly share loads of data about themselves, without knowing it, and then we'll cover collaborative filtering.

Whether you realize it or not, you interact with numerous recommender systems on a daily basis. If you've ever purchased from Amazon, or browsed on Facebook, or watched a show on Netflix, you've been served some form of personalized content. This is how e-commerce platforms maximize conversion rates and keep you coming back for more.

One of the marks of a really good recommender system is that it knows what you want whether you already know it or not. A good one will make you really wonder: how did they know that? So, it turns out that humans are extraordinarily predictable in their behavior, even without having to share information about themselves, and we call that voting with our feet, meaning that a user may profess to enjoy one genre of movie, say comedy, but disproportionately consume another, say romance. So, the goal of a recommender system is simply to get you to bite; However, the secondary goal generally differs based on the platform itself. It could be to maximize revenue for the seller, create satisfaction for the customer, or any number of other metrics. But what really makes these so interesting is that they're directly consumable by human beings, whereas so many other **machine learning** (**ML**) models exist to replace an automated process.

Here's an example, explaining voting with your feet:

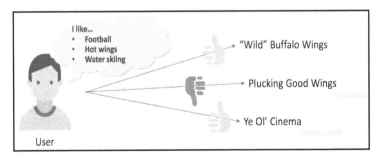

This user says he likes football, hot wings, and water skiing. And yet his ratings history shows that he's thumbed up one wing restaurant, thumbed down another, and then thumbed up a movie cinema. So, what this means is that there's something about the second wing restaurant that he didn't like. Maybe it was the ambiance, or maybe it was a wing sauce. Whatever it was, his interest in hot wings—his professed interest in hot wings—is more nuanced than he originally led us to believe. And, likewise, he's expressed an interest in movies, even though he's not disclosed it. So, the point here is that people say more with their actions than they do with their words, and they're more honest with their actions than they are with their words. We can exploit that with recommender systems to learn these nuanced patterns between items and people's interests.

Collaborative filtering is a common family of recommender systems. It's based on a concept known as **homophily**, which is basically *birds of a feather flock together*. So, that is, if you like something, people who also like that item probably share some other common interests with you; now we have a good pool of interest to start recommending things to one another.

In a typical collaborative filtering system, this is the format our data is going to resemble:

	Wing Store A	Wing Store B	Classic Sub Shop	The Burger Joint	The Salad Place	The Sports Bar	Steak House	Craft Brewery
	5.0	1.0			2.5	4.5		
			3.5	2.0	3.0			
	1.5				4.0		4.5	4.0
	?	1.0	?	?	1.0	?	?	5.0

In the preceding screenshot, users are shown along the y axis—which are rows—and items are shown along the x axis—which are columns. You might have explicit ratings, which are usually continuous along this continuum, or implicit, which are commonly binary. What we're showing here is explicit. The question we seek to answer is what's the predicted rating for a user? But to get there, we have to somehow compute the similarities between the items. This is a form of collaborative filtering called item-to-item collaborative filtering, and we can only compute similarities between the items that have been mutually rated by a user. This usually works best for explicitly rated systems; it's based on a paper that was published by Amazon several years ago.

Computing similarities between items is straightforward. We can compute pairwise similarities using one of several common metrics, including the **Pearson correlation** or cosine similarity. For example, we're going to use cosine similarity as follows:

$$cossim(x, y) = \frac{xy}{\|x\|_2 \|y\|_2}$$

It's computed in a very similar fashion to what we looked at with clustering in `Chapter 3`,*Working with Non-Parametric Models*, the **Euclidean distance**. However, this is computing similarity rather than spatial distance. So, it's the exact inverse of the concept, but computed in a similar fashion.

Since our data is so sparse, we're going to start out by putting it into a sparse CSR matrix using SciPy, and rather than having to store 32 elements, now we only have to store 14:

```
from scipy import sparse
import numpy as np

rows = np.array([0,0,0,0,1,1,1,2,2,2,2,3,3,3])
cols = np.array([0,1,4,5,2,3,4,0,4,6,7,1,4,7])
data = np.array([5.,1.,2.5,4.5,3.5,2.,3.,1.5,
                 4.,4.5,4.,1.,1.,5.])
# Make a sparse matrix
R = sparse.csr_matrix((data, (rows, cols)), shape = (4, 8))
print(R.todense())
```

The output of the preceding code is as follows:

```
[[5.  1.  0.  0.  2.5 4.5 0.  0. ]
 [0.  0.  3.5 2.  3.  0.  0.  0. ]
 [1.5 0.  0.  0.  4.  0.  4.5 4. ]
 [0.  1.  0.  0.  1.  0.  0.  5. ]]
```

This is a dense matrix based on what we would actually see. So, you can imagine how handy this becomes when we have thousands of users and millions of items—as Amazon does, for instance.

We're simply going to compute the pairwise cosine similarities of the transpose of the matrix. We have a lot of zeros in here. It's not that a lot of these are orthogonal, which, mathematically, is what a cosine similarity would represent with a zero; it's that we're experiencing something called the item cold start, where there are several items that have never been mutually rated together. And, therefore, we cannot effectively compute the similarity on the basis of ratings alone.

Now we will see how to generate predictions for a given user giving their history in the computed items similarities. In the following example, we are using the same user and we're just predicting for user_3:

```
from sklearn.metrics.pairwise import cosine_similarity

# Compute the sim matrix
sim = cosine_similarity(R.T).round(3)
sim
top_k = 3
user_3 = np.array([0., 1., 0., 0., 1., 0., 0., 5.])

# compute dot product btwn user vec and the sim matrix
recommendations = user_3.dot(sim)
item_indices = np.arange(recommendations.shape[0])

# now arg sort descending (most similar items first)
order = np.argsort(-recommendations)[:top_k]
items = item_indices[order]

# zip them together (item, predicted rating)
list(zip(items, recommendations[order]))
```

The output of the preceding code is as follows:

```
[(7, 6.130000000000001), (4, 4.326), (1, 4.196)]
```

So, computing predictions is easy enough in this algorithm. You just compute the dot product of that user's ratings vector and the similarities matrix. Then, `argsort` it to descending order, in a very similar fashion to how we did with nearest neighbors, but the inverse in terms of descending versus ascending. So, there are things to note here. First, the predicted rating exceeds the scale of the ground truth rating of 6.12. We only rated up to five, but we can't guarantee bounded ratings. So, we could either call those ratings or use some other strategy, but the other two ratings are actually the ones that the user has rated before. If you look back to the ratings matrix, both of these were rated as one star by the user. So, we can see that this is not a great recommender model with its low rank and low number of users.

Recommender systems are technically supervised learning, but they differ in the traditional sense of the *x*, *y* pairing since our ground truth is technically our data itself. So, in our example, we could look at the ratings for item four and one, and say how far we were off from the ground truth.

Item-to-item collaborative filtering

Let's look at the code. This is item-to-item collaborative filtering. Let's start with the `base.py` file that is present in `packtml/recommendation`:

```
class RecommenderMixin(six.with_metaclass(ABCMeta)):
    """Mixin interface for recommenders.

    This class should be inherited by recommender algorithms. It provides
an
    abstract interface for generating recommendations for a user, and a
    function for creating recommendations for all users.
    """
    @abstractmethod
    def recommend_for_user(self, R, user, n=10,
filter_previously_seen=False,
                             return_scores=True, **kwargs):
        """Generate recommendations for a user.

        A method that should be overridden by subclasses to create
        recommendations via their own prediction strategy.
        """

    def recommend_for_all_users(self, R, n=10,
                                 filter_previously_seen=False,
                                 return_scores=True, **kwargs):
        """Create recommendations for all users."""
        return (
```

```
            self.recommend_for_user(
                    R, user, n=n,
        filter_previously_seen=filter_previously_seen,
                    return_scores=return_scores, **kwargs)
            for user in xrange(R.shape[0]))
```

This `base` class is called `RecommenderMixin`. It's simply an interface. There are two methods: one is already written for all subclasses, and that's `recommend_for_all_users`; the other is `recommended_for_user`. So, we need to override it based on the subclass. The subclass we're going to look at is item-to-item collaborative filtering.

In the following `itemitem.py` file, we see two parameters:

```
    def __init__(self, R, k=10):
            # check the array, but don't copy if not needed
            R = check_array(R, dtype=np.float32, copy=False) # type: np.ndarray

            # save the hyper param for later use later
            self.k = k
            self.similarity = self._compute_sim(R, k)

    def _compute_sim(self, R, k):
            # compute the similarity between all the items. This calculates the
            # similarity between each ITEM
            sim = cosine_similarity(R.T)

            # Only keep the similarities of the top K, setting all others to
zero
            # (negative since we want descending)
            not_top_k = np.argsort(-sim, axis=1)[:, k:] # shape=(n_items, k)

            if not_top_k.shape[1]: # only if there are cols (k < n_items)
                # now we have to set these to zero in the similarity matrix
                row_indices = np.repeat(range(not_top_k.shape[0]),
                                        not_top_k.shape[1])
                sim[row_indices, not_top_k.ravel()] = 0.

            return sim

    def recommend_for_user(self, R, user, n=10,
                            filter_previously_seen=False,
                            return_scores=True, **kwargs):
            """Generate predictions for a single user.
```

We have R and k. R, which is our ratings matrix, it is different from other base estimators in that we don't have the corresponding y value. R is our ground truth as well as the training array. k is a parameter that we can use to limit the top number of items that are similar. It helps reduce our space that we're comparing within and makes computations easier. So, for the constructor, the fit procedure is simply computing the similarity array via the compute_sim function. We take the R array, transpose it so items are along the row axis, and then we compute the cosine similarity between the rows, which are now the items. We have an *n x n* matrix, the first *n* stands for the November matrix and the second *n* is the dimensionality of the number of items. Basically, we're going to say anything that's not in top_k, we'll set to zero similarity. One of the strategies here is that it allows us to augment our similarity matrix in a way that, otherwise, we couldn't. And that's what we're doing: argsorting into the descending order. We want the most similar first, argsorting along the columns. We take the similarity matrix and store that in self.similarity. And we're going to use that when we compute predictions.

So, recommend_for_user is the function that we have to override in the super abstract interface. We can take several arguments. So, we have the user vector, which is an index, and *n*, which is the number of recommendations we want to produce. Now we get user_vector out of R:

```
# check the array and get the user vector
R = check_array(R, dtype=np.float32, copy=False)
user_vector = R[user, :]
```

The recommendations—the raw recommendations—are the inner products between the user vector and the similarity matrix, which produces an *nD* or *1D* array in NumPy.

We get item_indices with the help of an arange method in NumPy:

```
# compute the dot product between the user vector and the similarity
# matrix
recommendations = user_vector.dot(self.similarity) # shape=(n_items,)

# if we're filtering previously-seen items, now is the time to do that
item_indices = np.arange(recommendations.shape[0])
if filter_previously_seen:
    rated_mask = user_vector != 0.
    recommendations = recommendations[~rated_mask]
    item_indices = item_indices[~rated_mask]
```

We're going to order this based on the descending argsort of the recommendations. Now we can limit them to the top n if we want to.

If you want to produce recommendations for everything, you can just pass None as n. We're going to return items, indices, and recommendations, which are the predicted ratings for each of those corresponding items, as shown here:

```
# now arg sort descending (most similar items first)
order = np.argsort(-recommendations)[:n]
items = item_indices[order]

if return_scores:
    return items, recommendations[order]
return items
```

We go to the example_item_item_recommender.py file. We'll load up the interestingly titled dataset called get_completely_fabricated_ratings_data, which is available in the data.py file. Here, we've several users, as shown in the following code:

```
    return (np.array([
        # user 0 is a classic 30-yo millennial who is nostalgic for the 90s
        [5.0, 3.5, 5.0, 0.0, 0.0, 0.0, 4.5, 3.0,
         0.0, 2.5, 4.0, 4.0, 0.0, 1.5, 3.0],

        # user 1 is a 40-yo who only likes action
        [1.5, 0.0, 0.0, 1.0, 0.0, 4.0, 5.0, 0.0,
         2.0, 0.0, 3.0, 3.5, 0.0, 4.0, 0.0],

        # user 2 is a 12-yo whose parents are strict about what she
watches.
        [4.5, 4.0, 5.0, 0.0, 0.0, 0.0, 0.0, 4.0,
         3.5, 5.0, 0.0, 0.0, 0.0, 0.0, 5.0],

        # user 3 has just about seen it all, and doesn't really care for
        # the goofy stuff. (but seriously, who rates the Goonies 2/5???)
        [2.0, 1.0, 2.0, 1.0, 2.5, 4.5, 4.5, 0.5,
         1.5, 1.0, 2.0, 2.5, 3.5, 3.5, 2.0],

        # user 4 has just opened a netflix account and hasn't had a chance
        # to watch too much
        [0.0, 0.0, 0.0, 0.0, 2.0, 0.0, 0.0, 0.0,
         0.0, 0.0, 0.0, 1.5, 4.0, 0.0, 0.0],
    ]), np.array(["Ghost Busters", "Ghost Busters 2",
                  "The Goonies", "Big Trouble in Little China",
                  "The Rocky Horror Picture Show", "A Clockwork Orange",
                  "Pulp Fiction", "Bill & Ted's Excellent Adventure",
                  "Weekend at Bernie's", "Dumb and Dumber", "Clerks",
                  "Jay & Silent Bob Strike Back", "Tron", "Total Recall",
                  "The Princess Bride" ]))
```

Let's say that user 0 is a classic 30-year-old millennial who loves the nostalgia of the 90s. So, they highly rate The Princess Bride, Ghost Busters, and Ghost Busters 2. User 1 is a 40-year-old who only likes action movies. So, they rated Die Hard and Pulp Fiction. User 2 is a 12-year-old whose parents are fairly strict, so we can assume that user 2 has not watched Pulp Fiction or anything like that. But user 2 has watched Ghost Busters, Ghost Busters 2, and The Goonies. And user 2 rated them all pretty highly. User 3 has seen it all. And user 4 has just opened a Netflix account and hasn't had the chance to watch too much. So, user 4 is probably going to be the one we're interested in producing recommendations for.

 All this is a NumPy array. We're returning a dense array. You can return this as a sparse array.

In the example_item_item_recommender.py file that is present in examples/recommendation, we're going to get the R ratings matrix and titles from get_completely_fabricated_ratings_data:

```
#
######################################################################
##
# Use our fabricated data set
R, titles = get_completely_fabricated_ratings_data()

#
######################################################################
##
# Fit an item-item recommender, predict for user 0
rec = ItemItemRecommender(R, k=3)
user0_rec, user_0_preds = rec.recommend_for_user(
    R, user=0, filter_previously_seen=True,
    return_scores=True)
```

We create a recommender item with k=3. We only retain the three most similar corresponding items for each of the items. And then we produce the recommendations for user 0.

Let's see what the top three rated movies are for user 0 if we run
the `example_item_item_recommender.py` file:

```
(packt-sml) test@test-Veriton-Series:~/Downloads/Hands-on-Supervised-Machine-Learning-with-Python-master/examples/recommendation$ pyt
hon example_item_item_recommender.py
User 0's top 3 rated movies are: ['Ghost Busters', 'The Goonies', 'Pulp Fiction']
User 0's top 3 recommended movies are: ['Big Trouble in Little China', 'A Clockwork Orange', 'The Rocky Horror Picture Show']
Mean average precision: 0.667
(packt-sml) test@test-Veriton-Series:~/Downloads/Hands-on-Supervised-Machine-Learning-with-Python-master/examples/recommendation$
```

User 0's top three rated movies are: `Ghost Busters`, `The Goonies`, and `Pulp Fiction`.
This means user 0 has rated `Ghost Busters` and `The Goonies` highly but has not rated
`Pulp Fiction`.

We can also see that the mean average precision is roughly 2/3. The mean average precision
is a metric that we're going to use for recommender systems. It actually comes out of the
information retrieval domain. It's not like, say, mean absolute error or mean squared error.
What we're doing is stating what proportion of the ones we recommend existed in the
ground truth set. In this case, it means which ones the user rated highly to begin with,
which shows that the ones we produced were pretty good.

Matrix factorization

In this section, we're going to look into recommender systems and introduce matrix
factorization techniques. In typical collaborative filtering problems, we have users along
one axis and items or offers along the other axis. We want to solve for the predicted rating
for a user for any given item, but to get there we have to somehow compute the affinity
between the users or the item. In the previous section, we looked at item-to-item
collaborative filtering, where we explicitly computed the similarity matrix using the cosine
similarity metric, but now we want to explore a method that's not going to explicitly
compare items to items or users to users.

Matrix factorization is a form of collaborative filtering that focuses on the intangibles of
products. At a conceptual level, every product or restaurant, for example, has intangibles
that cause you to like, dislike, or remain indifferent toward them. For example, for a
restaurant, maybe the atmosphere or the vibe you get outweighs the menu. Or, consider the
following statement: the food's terrible but the happy hour is great. In this case, we're
interested in learning the hidden or latent variables that underlie and manifest themselves
throughout patterns in the data.

Matrix factorization is going to allow us to discover these latent variables by decomposing our single ratings matrix into two low-rank matrices that, 2 when multiplied, approximate the original ratings matrix. Intuitively, we're learning about these hidden factors or latent variables and learning how our users and items score against them. As shown in the following diagram, one of the low-rank matrices maps the users' affinities for the discovered factors and the other maps that item's rankings on the factors:

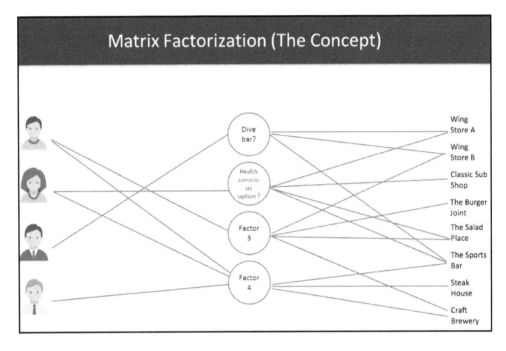

A drawback in matrix factorization is the lack of clarity or intuition behind what can make up a factor. It's similar to a **principal component** analysis (**PCA**) type technique, where a factor can be conceptualized as a topic. A careful, insightful analyst who has lots of subject matter expertise could feasibly extract meaning from topics, but it's very difficult to do so and, as a result, it's not typically pursued given its difficulty. For example, maybe **Factor 1** in the preceding diagram is a divey atmosphere. So, the wing shop is rated in varying degrees of divey-ness. As you can see on the right-hand side of the preceding diagram, there's a strong affinity between **Wing Store A** and the first factor, which is **Dive bar**. You can also assume that **The Sports Bar** might rate pretty highly on that scale. Then, perhaps **Factor 2** is a place that has some health-conscious options. So, the strength of that connection is the level at which a person or an offering ranks against the latent factor. You can see this on both the left-and the right-hand sides of the preceding diagram.

Essentially, we have a ratings matrix, Q. In different literature, it's referred to as either Q or R. We're going to call it Q here. We want to discover two lower rank matrices, X and Y, such that the product of the two approximate the ratings matrix. That is, Q or Q prime is approximately equal to $X.Y^T$:

$$Q = XY^T$$

$$X \in \mathbb{R}^{mxf} \quad Y \in \mathbb{R}^{nxf}$$

$$\min_{x,y} \sum_{r_{u,i}} (r_{u,i} - x_u^T y_i)^2 + \lambda(\sum_u \|x_u\|^2 + \sum_i \|y_i\|^2)$$

Our objective function is at the bottom and is basically a regularized mean squared error. So, we're looking at the mean squared error, or the reconstruction error, between X and Y and Q prime, and then we have the regularization term over on the other side, with lambda.

For the math folks, factorizing a matrix is nothing new. But doing so in the context of finding such low-rank matrices in a non-convex optimization problem might be a bit of a challenge. So, the approach we're going to see is called **Alternating Least Squares (ALS)**.

The ALS algorithm is as follows:

1. Initialize two random matrices, X and Y
2. Set empty values of Q and O
3. Beginning with X, solve the following:

$$X' = (Y^T Y + \lambda I)^{-1} Y^T Q$$

4. Now solve for Y with the new X:

$$Y' = (X^T X + \lambda I)^{-1} X^T Q$$

5. Iterate, alternating between X and Y until convergence

Essentially, we're going to alternate between solving each respective matrix with respect to the other, and we'll eventually reach a point of convergence. So, we start out by initializing both X and Y to random values. Then, starting with X, we solve for X prime. Now that we have a more refined version of X prime, we can use that to solve for Y prime. Each matrix creates a better solution for the other at each iteration. And we can alternate like this for as many iterations as we like, or until we hit a point of diminishing returns, where we would say that we've converged.

A quick note on the notation here: the *I* that you can see next to lambda is simply an *F x F* identity matrix, where *F* is the number of latent factors that we want to discover. We multiply that by the regularization parameter lambda. So, along the diagonal axis we have lambda, and then the rest is simply zeros.

Here's a hackneyed 30-line approximation of ALS in Python. We start out with defining Q or the ratings matrix:

```python
import numpy as np
from numpy.linalg import solve

nan = np.nan
Q = np.array([[5.0, 1.0, nan, nan, 2.5, 4.5, nan, nan],
              [nan, nan, 3.5, 2.0, 3.0, nan, nan, nan],
              [1.5, nan, nan, nan, 4.0, nan, 4.5, 4.0],
              [nan, 1.0, nan, nan, 1.0, nan, nan, 5.0]])

nan_mask = np.isnan(Q) # mask applied when computing loss
Q[nan_mask] = 0.

f = 3 # num factors
n_iter = 5 # num iterations
I_lambda = np.eye(f) * 0.01 # regularizing term
random_state = np.random.RandomState(42)

# initialize X, Y randomly
X = random_state.rand(Q.shape[0], f)
Y = random_state.rand(f, Q.shape[1])
W = nan_mask.astype(int) # weights for calculating loss (0/1)

# iterate:
errors = []
for i in range(n_iter):
    X = solve(Y.dot(Y.T) + I_lambda, Y.dot(Q.T)).T
    Y = solve(X.T.dot(X) + I_lambda, X.T.dot(Q))
    errors.append(((W * (Q - X.dot(Y))) ** 2).sum())
X.dot(Y).round(3)
```

This is the rating that we've seen in the earlier example, and in the previous section. Now we're going to get a Boolean mask, `nan_mask`. First, we're going to set all the missing values to zero for the ensuing computations. Next, we're going to initialize `I` as our identity matrix and multiply it by lambda. We only have to do that one time, which is nice. Lambda is just 0.01 for now, but that's a hyperparameter that can be tuned using cross-validation. So, the higher lambda is, the more we'll regularize. Then, we initialize `X` and `Y` with `random_state`. `X` is going to be equal to *M x F*, that is, the number of users by the number of factors. `Y` is going to be equal to the number of factors by the number of items: *F x N*.

In iterating, we solve for `X`, and then we solve for `Y` given the new `X`. Then, we compute our training loss, which is again the masked version of the mean squared error, where we mask out the missing values from the original ground truth array, which is our ratings array. And then we continue to iterate until we reach convergence.

At the bottom of the preceding code, you can see the output of the approximation between `X` and `Y`. It is an approximation. If you look at the definition of Q, 3 and then the output at the bottom, it looks pretty similar. So, the way that we would create predictions at the end is that we exploit the error in the whole system, and return the highest predicted items for a user filtering the previously rated ones. So, user 4, (the very last user), would get a recommendation for the steakhouse that is *2.0*, and this is the highest non-previously rated item for that user. This is actually just a result of the multiplication error or the approximation error.

In the following graph, you can see how the training loss diminishes over each iteration:

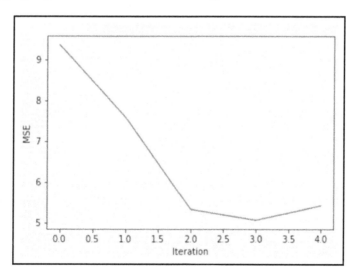

Matrix factorization in Python

In the previous section, we wanted to decompose our ratings matrix into two low-rank matrices in order to discover the intangible latent factors that drive consumers' decisions. One matrix maps the users' affinities for the discovered factors and the other maps the items' rankings on those factors.

So, let's look at how this can be implemented in Python. We've two files, `als.py` and `example_als_recommender`. Let's see our `als.py` file. In the last section, we saw the item-to-item collaborative filter; ALS is very similar. It's going to implement `RecommenderMixin`:

```
def __init__(self, R, factors=0.25, n_iter=10, lam=0.001,
    random_state=None):
```

We have several parameters for ALS. The first one, and the only non-optional one, is `R`, our ratings matrix. In some of the math we've seen, we've referred to this interchangeably as `R` and `Q`. Again, that's kind of a quirk of the literature. Depending on what papers you're reading, it's one or the other. And the second parameter we're going to take is `factors`.The `factors` parameter is the number of latent variables we want to discover. I have used float, but you can use an integer. The floating point is just going to be bound between zero and one. `n_iter` is the number of iterations. ALS, in this module, does not support early convergence or early stopping. That's something that you could absolutely write. But if you have too many iterations, what happens is you're probably going to overfit your data. Lambda is our regularization parameter, and then you can just pass `random_state` as a way for reproducibility.

For the first step, as always, we're going to check our array to make sure that we have only floating points:

```
# check the array
R = check_array(R, dtype=np.float32) # type: np.ndarray
n_users, n_items = R.shape
# get the random state
random_state = check_random_state(random_state)
```

We are going to allow missing data here, because missing data is natural in recommender systems. And we can almost guarantee there's always going to be missing data.

In the following code, we're making sure that our factor is an integer. And if it's `float`, we figure out the number of `factors` we're going to discover:

```
# get the number of factors. If it's a float, compute it
if isinstance(factors, float):
    factors = min(np.ceil(factors * n_items).astype(int), n_items)
```

So, `W` here is equal to `nan_mask`, which we looked at in the previous section:

```
W = (R > 0.).astype(np.float32)
```

This is going to be, essentially, a weighting array that says whether or not the value was missing to begin with. And so, we use this to mask our ground truth out of the ratings matrix when we compute our mean squared error during our iterations.

Here, we initialize `Y`:

```
# initialize the first array, Y, and X to None
 Y = random_state.rand(factors, n_items)
 X = None
# the identity matrix (time lambda) is added to the XX or YY product
# at each iteration.
 I = np.eye(factors) * lam
```

We are not initializing `X` because we know that that's going to be the first one we solve for in our iterations. So, as we have seen in the previous section, we also initialize `I` as the identity matrix—that is, *F x F*—and multiply it by our regularization parameter.

Now we're going to iterate, as shown in the following code:

```
# for each iteration, iteratively solve for X, Y, and compute the
# updated MSE
for i in xrange(n_iter):
 X = solve(Y.dot(Y.T) + I, Y.dot(R.T)).T
 Y = solve(X.T.dot(X) + I, X.T.dot(R))
# update the training error
 train_err.append(mse(R, X, Y, W))
# now we have X, Y, which are our user factors and item factors
 self.X = X
 self.Y = Y
 self.train_err = train_err
 self.n_factors = factors
 self.lam = lam
```

Begin by solving for `X`, and then solve for `Y`. At each iteration, we're going to just calculate the training error, which is the mean squared error. We append it to the list that we store as a `self` parameter in the following code.

The training phase is actually extraordinarily easy for ALS. Now, in the previous, section we didn't see how to concretely generate predictions. We saw the math behind it, but we haven't implemented it. If you call predict on ALS, as shown in the following code, it's simply going to compute the product of the user factors and the item factors to return the R prime—basically the approximation:

```
def predict(self, R, recompute_users=False):
        """Generate predictions for the test set.

        Computes the predicted product of ``XY`` given the fit factors.
        If recomputing users, will learn the new user factors given the
        existing item factors.
        """
        R = check_array(R, dtype=np.float32, copy=False) # type: np.ndarray
        Y = self.Y # item factors
        n_factors, _ = Y.shape

        # we can re-compute user factors on their updated ratings, if we
want.
        # (not always advisable, but can be useful for offline
recommenders)
        if recompute_users:
            I = np.eye(n_factors) * self.lam
            X = solve(Y.dot(Y.T) + I, Y.dot(R.T)).T
        else:
            X = self.X

        return X.dot(Y)
```

You can pass in R, which would ostensibly be the test data. This is the data to include new users who weren't included in the fit originally, or it could mean that the users have updated their data. But we can recompute the user factors if we want to. So, if the users have moved on in time and our fit is about a week old, then we can recompute the user factors with respect to the existing item factors. Then, at the end, we're just returning the product of X and Y.

Now we'll call the recommend_for_user function. So, given your test matrix and the user index, we want to know what the top n items are to recommend for a user and we do largely the same thing:

```
def recommend_for_user(self, R, user, n=10, recompute_user=False,
                       filter_previously_seen=False,
                       return_scores=True):
```

We're going to create this prediction, but extract out the predicted user vector. So, we're using the `self.predict` method, as shown in the following code:

```
R = check_array(R, dtype=np.float32, copy=False)
# compute the new user vector. Squeeze to make sure it's a vector
 user_vec = self.predict(R, recompute_users=recompute_user)[user, :]
 item_indices = np.arange(user_vec.shape[0])
# if we are filtering previously seen, remove the prior-rated items
 if filter_previously_seen:
 rated_mask = R[user, :] != 0.
 user_vec = user_vec[~rated_mask]
 item_indices = item_indices[~rated_mask]
order = np.argsort(-user_vec)[:n] # descending order of computed scores
 items = item_indices[order]
 if return_scores:
 return items, user_vec[order]
 return items
```

If we are interested in filtering out the ones we previously saw, we just mask those out and return the descending argsorted indices of items that we're interested in. This is very similar to what we've seen before when we were looking at spatial clustering, but here, all we're doing is computing the approximation of X and Y and argsorting the columns.

Let's look at an example in the `example_als_recommender.py` file:

```
# -*- coding: utf-8 -*-

from __future__ import absolute_import

from packtml.recommendation import ALS
from packtml.recommendation.data import
get_completely_fabricated_ratings_data
from packtml.metrics.ranking import mean_average_precision
from matplotlib import pyplot as plt
import numpy as np
import sys


#
###############################################################################
##
# Use our fabricated data set
R, titles = get_completely_fabricated_ratings_data()

#
###############################################################################
##
# Fit an item-item recommender, predict for user 0
```

```
n_iter = 25
rec = ALS(R, factors=5, n_iter=n_iter, random_state=42, lam=0.01)
user0_rec, user_0_preds = rec.recommend_for_user(
    R, user=0, filter_previously_seen=True,
    return_scores=True)

# print some info about user 0
top_rated = np.argsort(-R[0, :])[:3]
print("User 0's top 3 rated movies are: %r" % titles[top_rated].tolist())
print("User 0's top 3 recommended movies are: %r"
      % titles[user0_rec[:3]].tolist())
```

You may recall from the preceding code the recommended data. This is the completely fabricated data that we went on about in the previous sections. We're going to take this same data and we're going to fit ALS on it. We want to know user 0's predictions, so, before we run it, we need some information. Let's say user 0 rated `Ghost Busters` pretty highly, and rated `The Goonies` pretty highly as well. This guy knows their stuff! So, this guy is a classic 90s/late 80s millennial.

You'll notice, in the following screenshot, that we have activated my `packt-sml` conda environment:

```
(packt-sml) test@test-Veriton-Series:~/Downloads/Hands-on-Supervised-Machine-Learning-with-Python-master/examples/recommendation$ pyt
hon example_als_recommender.py
User 0's top 3 rated movies are: ['Ghost Busters', 'The Goonies', 'Pulp Fiction']
User 0's top 3 recommended movies are: ["Weekend at Bernie's", 'A Clockwork Orange', 'Tron']
Mean average precision: 0.667
```

The output of the preceding code is as follows:

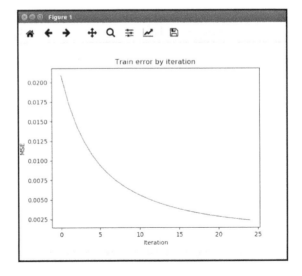

You need to do the same. So, when we run this, we'll get the preceding graph, which is showing how the training error diminishes over the iterations, as we expect it would. As a result, we would recommend that user 0 watch `Weekend at Bernie's` as the top-rated suggestion. And that seems to make sense given `The Goonies` and `Ghost Busters`. But then `Pulp Fiction` is a bit violent, and so we also recommended `Clockwork Orange`, which also seems to jive with that. So, the mean average precision is, essentially, looking at the recommendations and then comparing them to the ground truth and saying how many of those were actually previously rated highly.

Limitations of ALS

We've been using explicit ratings. For example, on Amazon, ratings are between one and five stars. The problem here is that explicit rating systems typically have trouble getting users to rate the items, because it's easier to consume that content than it is to evaluate it from the user side. So, implicit ratings are the inverse of explicit ratings and they can be collected by a system, usually, without the user's awareness. A lot of times that's more favorable, because it doesn't require the user to interact with the system in a secondary sense to explicitly rate items, and we can get more data, which means less sparse data. So, implicit ratings might include the number of listens to a song. There's really well-known ratings dataset collected by the Last FM team that uses implicit ratings, and it's commonly used for benchmarking recommender systems. There is an implicit variation of ALS, but we only covered the explicit version. But if you check on Google for implicit ALS, there's all sorts of literature around it. We encourage you to go look it up.

The next challenge of recommenders is sparsity versus density. As we've seen, ratings matrices can be pretty sparse. For some systems, such as Amazon, there may only be ratings for less than approximately one percent of all items per user, and a lot of times even less than that. So, dense matrices are not usually the best solution, and oftentimes they're not even feasible. So, we either have to use sparse matrices or get really clever with how we distribute the data, so we don't totally blow up our memory.

Recommenders typically take a very long time to train. Like many other machine learning models, we run into that same kind of thing, but recommenders are a bit different in the sense that they have to be updated in much greater frequency, in many cases, multiple times per day, depending on the system itself. So, new items arriving in a catalog or new users beginning to consume media means that the recommender has to be refreshed. But we can't do this online or in real time, or we risk taking the system down. So, generally, recommenders are retrained on a periodic basis in an offline fashion. And the models are scored in an online or more real-time fashion.

In this section, we looked at the Python implementation of ALS in the `packtml` library and an example. Finally, we discussed some of the real-world challenges we face in recommender systems.

Content-based filtering

In this section, we're going to wrap up our discussion around recommender systems by introducing an entirely separate approach to computing similarities and look at how we can use it to augment our collaborative filtering systems.

Content-based recommenders operate similarly to the original item-to-item collaborative system that we saw earlier, but they don't use ratings data to compute the similarities. Instead, they compute the similarities directly by using provided attributes of the items in the catalog. Predictions can then be computed in the same fashion as item-to-item collaborative filtering by calculating the product of the ratings matrix and similarity matrix.

Here's an example of how we might use content vectors to directly compute the item similarity matrix:

```python
import numpy as np
from sklearn.metrics.pairwise import cosine_similarity

ratings = np.array(([5.0, 1.0, 0.0, 0.0, 2.5, 4.5, 0.0, 0.0],
                    [0.0, 0.0, 3.5, 2.0, 3.0, 0.0, 0.0, 0.0],
                    [1.5, 0.0, 0.0, 0.0, 4.0, 0.0, 4.5, 4.0],
                    [0.0, 1.0, 0.0, 0.0, 1.0, 0.0, 0.0, 5.0]))
# content vector

categories = ['Alcohol license',
              'Healthy options',
              'Burgers on menu',
              'Located in downtown',
              '$', '$$', '$$$', '$$$$',
              'Full bar', 'Southern cooking',
              'Grilled food']
# categories      a1  he  bu  dt  1$  2$  3$  4$  fb  sc  gf
content = np.array([[0., 1., 0., 0., 0., 1., 0., 0., 0., 0., 0.],
                    [1., 0., 1., 1., 0., 1., 0., 0., 1., 0., 0.],
                    [0., 1., 1., 0., 1., 0., 0., 0., 0., 0., 1.],
                    [1., 1., 1., 1., 0., 0., 1., 0., 0., 1., 1.],
                    [0., 1., 0., 0., 1., 0., 0., 0., 0., 0., 1.],
                    [1., 0., 1., 0., 0., 0., 1., 0., 0., 1., 1.],
                    [1., 1., 0., 1., 0., 0., 0., 1., 1., 0., 1.],
```

```
                    [1., 1., 1., 0., 0., 0., 1., 0., 0., 0., 1.]
                    ])
sim = cosine_similarity(content)
ratings.dot(sim).round(3)
```

The output of the preceding code is as follows:

```
array([[6.337, 4.381, 6.169, 6.738, 5.703, 5.545, 4.813, 6.872],
       [2.997, 1.797, 7.232, 5.294, 6.904, 4.03 , 4.078, 5.587],
       [5.697, 4.539, 8.515, 8.305, 8.799, 5.876, 9.01 , 9.005],
       [2.306, 3.  , 4.444, 5.169, 3.582, 4.658, 3.758, 5.916]])
```

We're using the same ratings matrix as we have over the last few sections, and we've created 11 different attributes about the various restaurants. Generally, the content vectors of these dummy-encoded features indicate whether an item belongs to a given category. So, you can see the similarity is computed in exactly the same fashion. So, we just compute the cosine similarity between the rows. And then we even generate predictions in the same way. We compute the product of the similarities and the ratings.

Limitations of content-based systems

There are several notable limitations to content-based systems that make them less than ideal in most scenarios. The first of these is the manual nature of the feature engineering, which can be extraordinarily tough given that the difficulty of collecting the data about the items can be really time-consuming, and many times, the data we're presented about an item is limited to a text description. So, we're not given this nice encoded matrix and that means we have to extract the attributes from descriptions, which can be challenging and extremely time-intensive.

Next, we end up with the largely dummy-encoded set of content vectors, meaning it's heavily zero inflated. So, naturally, our similarity computations are going to be fairly low with respect to what we might get out of a comparable collaborative approaches computation. And, finally, as our feature matrix grows in rank, the similarity between the two given items will be orthogonal or zero, so the likelihood of that approaches 1. For more information, you can refer to https://math.stackexchange.com/questions/995623/why-are-randomly-drawn-vectors-nearly-perpendicular-in-high-dimensions. It's a loose proof showing that the higher the rank, the more likely it is that you approach that orthogonality, which we don't want. All these limitations make a good case for why content-based systems are less favorable than collaboratively based systems.

But there're also some cases where they can be really useful. One of these is called the **cold-start problem**, which we discussed earlier in this section, and we encounter in every collaborative filtering application. This is when a new item is added and it cannot be compared to an existing item on the basis of ratings due to its own lack of ratings. So, the challenge here, apart from being unable to compute that similarity, is that if you impute it with a 0 or some other random value, you may never present that to a consumer. You implicitly diminish the chance that you would ever recommend that item.

In item-to-item collaborative filtering, it also occurs in situations where there are two items that have not been mutually rated by the same user, since we can't compute the similarity. So, that's an additional case and, in this one, it's going to result in a similarity of 0 in our matrix because we impute all the missing values with 0, even though we, theoretically, have ratings on which to gauge the affinity. In these scenarios, it's useful to have a fallback plan.

Here, we're fitting an item-to-item collaborative filtering recommender:

```
from packtml.recommendation import ItemItemRecommender

rec = ItemItemRecommender(ratings, k=5)

zero_mask = rec.similarity == 0
rec.similarity[zero_mask] = sim[zero_mask]
rec.similarity
```

The output of the preceding code is as follows:

```
array([[0.99999994, 0.67728543, 0.35355338, 0.26726124, 0.62405604,
        0.95782626, 0.28734788, 0.31622776],
       [0.67728543, 0.99999994, 0.2236068 , 0.50709254, 0.43580094,
        0.70710677, 0.5477226 , 0.5521576 ],
       [0.35355338, 0.2236068 , 1. , 1. , 0.52827054,
        0.4472136 , 0.4082483 , 0.6708204 ],
       [0.26726124, 0.50709254, 1. , 1. , 0.52827054,
        0.8451542 , 0.6172134 , 0.8451542 ],
       [0.62405604, 0. , 0.52827054, 0.4364358 , 1. ,
        0.2581989 , 0.7043607 , 0.577514 ],
       [0.95782626, 0.70710677, 0.4472136 , 0.8451542 , 0.44022545,
        1. , 0.36514837, 0.8 ],
       [0.28734788, 0.5477226 , 0.4082483 , 0.6172134 , 0.7043607 ,
        0.36514837, 1. , 0.62469506],
       [0.1795048 , 0.5521576 , 0.6708204 , 0.8451542 , 0.577514 ,
        0.8 , 0.62469506, 0.99999994]], dtype=float32)
```

From preceding code, we see several sections from the `packtml` package on our ratings data, which we've been using for the last few sections. We're going to use the content similarity computations to impute the data that suffers from the cold-start problem. When we examine the similarity matrix, you can see that there are no more 0s. So, there is a corner case where you might get a 0, and that's if you had a missing mutual similarity or a cold-start problem, and then perfect orthogonality in the actual content vectors. But we don't see that. So, ostensibly, this gets us closer to a more robust model. But you're still restricted to the limitations that we have seen before, namely, collecting the content attributes and computing those potentially orthogonal vectors.

So, at this point, you're familiar with the concept and you realize content-based similarities alone are not very feasible. But they can actually augment your collaborative filtering method if you have the right situation and setup. There's been a lot of research around using neural networks to automatically hybridize content-based and collaborative systems. A lot of them are using neural networks to create features from text descriptions a touch informal in an automatic sense, and then creating a separate network to factorize the matrices. So, there's a lot of hope in the future that content and collaborative systems can exist in parity.

The following are two papers that are pursuing this approach:

- *Hybrid Collaborative Filtering with Neural Networks*, Florian Strub, Jeremie Mary, and Romaric Gaudel, 2016
- *Hybrid Recommender System Using Semi-supervised Clustering Based on Gaussian Mixture Model*, Cyberworlds (CW), 2016 International Conference, pp. 155-158, 2016

Neural networks and deep learning

This is a huge topic in machine learning, so we can't cover everything in this chapter. If you've never seen a neural network before, they look like a giant spider web. The vertices of these spider webs are called neurons, or units, and they are based on an old-school linear classifier known as a perceptron. The idea is that your vector comes in, computes a dot product with a corresponding weight vector of parameters, and then gets a bias value added to it. Then, we transform it via an activation function. A perceptron, in general, can be canonically the same as logistic regression if you're using a sigmoid transformation.

When you string a whole bunch of these together, what you get is the massive web of perceptrons feeding perceptrons: this is called a multi layer perceptron, but it's also known as a neural network. As each of these perceptrons feeds the next layer, the neurons end up learning a series of nonlinear transformations in the input space, ultimately producing a prediction in the final layer.

The history of these models is actually really fascinating. They were first proposed in the early 1950s, but their potential was not really unlocked for quite a long time, since they're so computationally intensive. Nowadays, though, we hear a bout deep learning everywhere, and it's really just referring to the broader family of neural networks, including some of their unsupervised and generative variants.

So, how does a neural network actually learn? Well, we're going to iteratively feed the data through layers of the networks in epochs. Feeding the layer forward is as simple as computing a matrix product between one layer and the next, adding the bias vector along the column axis, and then transforming the output via the activation function. There are a lot of different activation functions you can use, but some of the most common ones are the sigmoid; the hyperbolic tangent, which is similar to the sigmoid but bounds between negative one and one rather than zero and one; and **rectified linear units** (**ReLUs**), which really are just flooring functions between the value and zero. It makes sure that nothing negative comes out of the units. So, after each epoch or iteration, outside the output layer we're going to compute the error of the network, and pass the message back up through the layers and they can adjust their weights accordingly. This process is called backpropagation. We usually use gradient descent for this.

For our two-layer example, which is really just a single layer in the middle with an output layer at the end, we only have to compute two matrix products for each epoch. It's been found that how you initialize your weights makes a huge difference in the capacity for the network to learn. There are several approaches to the strategies for this, but the easiest way is to just initialize them to very small values. We typically pick random values between negative and positive 0.1. You can go smaller; you can get more clever. We will initialize our biases as 1 vectors. Again, there are other clever ways to do this. We're just going to use 1, and the weight matrices themselves map one layer to the next. So, going from layer 1 to layer 2, we go from three units to four. You can see that dimensionality in the number of units. Our corresponding weight matrix is going to be *3 x 4* and, likewise, for the second one it's going to be *4 x 2*.

Here, we're just expressing our network as a system of linear equations:

$$f(f(XW_1 + b_1 W_2 + b_2) = \mathbb{R}^{m \times 2}$$

The first layer is passed to the second layer in that nested parentheses on the inside, and then to the last layer on the outer parentheses. And what we end up with is this real matrix in *m x 2*.

Here's a forward pass in a snippet of highly oversimplified Python code:

```python
import numpy as np

# define activation function
f = (lambda v: 1./ (1. + np.exp(-v)))
lam = 0.01
# input matrix
X = np.array([[1.5, 5.0, 2.5],
              [0.6, 3.5, 2.8],
              [2.4, 5.6, 5.6]])

y = np.array([1, 1, 0])
# initialize hidden layers, bias

rs = np.random.RandomState(42)
H1 = rs.rand(3, 4)
H2 = rs.rand(4, 2)
b1, b2 = np.ones(4), np.ones(2)

# feed forward
H1_res = f(X.dot(H1) + b1)
output = f(H1_res.dot(H2) + b2)
```

We're defining our activation function. `f` is a logistic or sigmoid transformation. `lam`, or `lambda`, is going to be our learning rate, which we learned about when we talked about gradient descent. And you'll remember this from logistic regression, where we can control the rate of how we descend that gradient. After initializing `X` and `y`, which we're just using as random values, we create hidden `H1` and `H2` layers, and `b1` and `b2` biases. In this example, we created the layers using the NumPy `rand` function. But this is where you'd want to get clever and bound them between negative `0.1` and `0.1` on the positive scale. Then, the result of our hidden layer one, `H1_res`, is computed by applying our `f` activation function to the `AX + b` linear equation. So, we just compute the inner product between `X` and `H1`, and then add the bias vector along the column vectors.

The output is computed by applying the second hidden layer to the output of the first in the same fashion. So, we're chaining these linear systems into one another, and applying this nonlinear transformation to that output.

So, now that we have our first epoch complete, we need to adjust the weights of the network to get an error-minimizing state because, right now, the chances are our network produced a terrible error. And so, here begins the fun of backpropagation, and if you thought we had a lot of calculus earlier in this book, you're in for a treat here. We're going to compute four derivatives: two for each layer. We use them to adjust the weight in the layer immediately above, much like we did in logistic regression. Then, the next time we do a forward pass, the weights have been adjusted and we'll, in theory, have less error in the network than we did previously.

Here, we're implementing backpropagation from scratch:

```
# back prop
out_delta = output.copy() # get a copy of the output
out_delta[range(X.shape[0]), y] -= 1.
H2_d = H1_res.T.dot(out_delta)
b2_d = H2_d.sum(axis=0)
delta2 = out_delta.dot(H2.T) * (1. - np.power(H1_res, 2.))
H1_d = X.T.dot(delta2)
b1_d = delta2.sum(axis=0)

# update weights, bias

H1 += -lam * H1_d
b1 += -lam * b1_d
H2 += -lam * H2_d
b2 += -lam * b2_d
```

We're going to compute four derivatives: the derivative and loss function with respect to each of the weights layers—that's two—and the bias layers—that's another two. The first delta is really easy to compute: it's simply the predicted probabilities, which is this matrix minus the truth indices of `y`. Next, we're going to compute the first layer's output with the delta we just computed, which is going to be a derivative with respect to the last layer, which is the output layer. And, after that, we can sum along the columns of our results to get the derivative of our second layer biases.

We can use the same process to compute our derivatives for the next `H1` and `b1` layer. Once we have those gradients computed, we can update the weights and biases in the same fashion as we did in logistic regression, which is by multiplying each derivative by the negative learning rate, and adding that to the weights matrices and `H1` and `b1`, and `H2` and `b2` bias vectors, respectively. And now we've updated our weights and biases along the axis of greatest change in our function: the loss function.

So, if you backpropagate correctly, you're going to get error terms that converge similarly to the following graph:

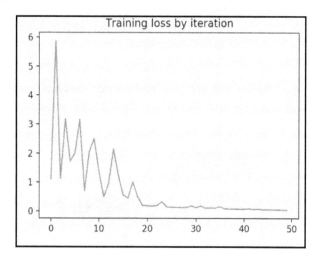

Tips and tricks for training a neural network

Here are some tricks that can make your life easier when you're actually training a neural network from scratch. You can stop your training a bit early to avoid overfitting. In the preceding graph, you can see there's a long tail where the error does not decrease anymore and we're still training. It's at a point around epoch 25 or 30. We could have stopped early.

Regularization and dropout are ways that can prevent your network from overfitting. Now, for extremely large data, you can do partial fits per epoch, meaning that you can fit many batches through your network for each forward pass so that you don't have to hold everything in memory. It also makes backpropagation a little easier, and different activation functions are going to give you different results. So, always try them out. And, finally, always use cross-validation, as we've talked about before, to select your model hyperparameters, so that you don't inadvertently create model leakage with the validation set, or even with overfitting your training set.

Neural networks

We're going to iteratively feed the data through layers in the network in epochs. After each iteration, we're going to compute the error of the network and the output, and pass the signal back up through the layers so they can adjust their weights accordingly. So, that's all for the theory and recaps.

We have two files we're going to look at. We have the source code and an example: `base.py` and `mlp.py`, which stands for multilayer perceptron. Let's start with `base.py`:

```
def tanh(X):
    """Hyperbolic tangent.

    Compute the tan-h (Hyperbolic tangent) activation function.
    This is a very easily-differentiable activation function.

    Parameters
    ----------
    X : np.ndarray, shape=(n_samples, n_features)
        The transformed X array (X * W + b).
    """
    return np.tanh(X)


class NeuralMixin(six.with_metaclass(ABCMeta)):
    """Abstract interface for neural network classes."""
    @abstractmethod
    def export_weights_and_biases(self, output_layer=True):
        """Return the weights and biases of the network"""
```

We have two functions. One function, `tanh`, is a hyperbolic tangent function we're going to use as our activation function. And this is just a wrapper for `np.tanh`. Then, we have a `NeuralMixin` class, which is kind of an abstract interface we're going to use for exporting the weights and biases of each of our networks.

In `mlp.py`, we're going to depend on the typical `check_X_y` from scikit-learn, `check_classification_targets`. Because we're only performing either binary or multiclass classification, we're going to use softmax, and then `check_random_state`. So, we can use a replicable `random_state` inside of our neural network.

There is a function outside of the class itself—`calculate_loss`:

```
def _calculate_loss(truth, preds, weights, l2):
    """Compute the log loss.

    Calculate the log loss between the true class labels and the
predictions
    generated by the softmax layer in our neural network.

    Parameters
    ----------
    truth : np.ndarray, shape=(n_samples,)
        The true labels

    preds : np.ndarray, shape=(n_samples, n_classes)
        The predicted class probabilities

    weights : list
        The list of weights matrices. Used for computing the loss
        with the L2 regularization.

    l2 : float
        The regularization parameter
    """
    # get the log probs of the prediction for the true class labels
    n_samples = truth.shape[0]
    logprobs = -np.log(preds[range(n_samples), truth])

    # compute the sum of log probs
    sum_logprobs = logprobs.sum()

    # add the L2 regularization term
    sum_logprobs += l2 / 2. * sum(np.square(W).sum() for W in weights)
    return 1. / n_samples * sum_logprobs
```

Essentially, this is going to be our objective function inside of our neural network that we can compute, and backpropagate that loss up through the network. Softmax is going to be the generalization, that is, our logistic function applied to multiple classes. So, that's what we get out of this. From the K matrix, where K is the dimension of the number of classes, we have a three-class problem; we can compute probabilities for the membership of each of those classes. And that's what softmax does.

Now our neural net classifier is going to take a number of different parameters, as shown here:

```
def __init__(self, X, y, hidden=(25,), n_iter=10, learning_rate=0.001,
             regularization=0.01, random_state=42):
```

As usual, we have our X and y, and then we have `hidden`, which is going to be a tuple or some other iterable that has positional elements indicating the number of units in each layer. So, if we wanted to have two layers, we might have X, 25, where each layer would have 25 units. There is no exact science to determining how many units you want and it kind of depends on your objective. If you want to compress the dimensionality, you might make the number of units smaller than the input dimensionality. If you want to discover all sorts of nuanced features, then you might expand the number of units. The number of iterations is actually the number of epochs we're going to perform. The learning rate is the lambda that we've seen in logistic regression. Regularization is our 12 penalty that's going to help us prevent overfitting. And `random_state`, again, is the seed that we'll use to control `random_state` so this is replicable.

In the constructor, all we're doing is self-assigning different attributes to the algorithm:

```
self.hidden = hidden
self.random_state = random_state
self.n_iter = n_iter
self.learning_rate = learning_rate
self.regularization = regularization
# initialize weights, biases, etc.
X, y, weights, biases = self._init_weights_biases(
    X, y, hidden, random_state, last_dim=None)
```

Then, we initialize the weights and biases. We're tracking the last dimension of the last matrix, or hidden weight matrix. So, we will start the input with none. We're going to use the column dimensionality as the input dimensionality of the next layer. So, we mentioned in the example that we went from three to four. Our dimensionality of the first hidden matrix or hidden layer may be *3 x 4*. We're tracking the last column dimensionality because that becomes the row dimensionality of the next layer. We return to X, y, `weights`, `biases`, and this will be used by subclasses later, as well, which is why it's a class function.

Now we start progressing through forward passes of our network. First, we compute the forward step:

```
def _forward_step(X, weights, biases):
    # track the intermediate products
    intermediate_results = [X]

    # progress through all the layers EXCEPT the very last one.
    for w, b in zip(weights[:-1], biases[:-1]):

        # apply the activation function to the product of X and the
weights
        # (after adding the bias vector)
        X = tanh(X.dot(w) + b)
```

```
        # append this layer result
        intermediate_results.append(X)

    # we handle the very last layer a bit differently, since it's out
    # output layer. First compute the product...
    X = X.dot(weights[-1]) + biases[-1]

    # then rather than apply the activation function (tanh), we apply
    # the softmax, which is essentially generalized logistic
regression.
        return softmax(X), intermediate_results
```

A forward step is pretty easy. We have X, our weights, and our biases. We're going to ZIP our weights and biases together so we can track them together. And we're just going to compute that product of X.dot(w), w being weight, and add biases. This is again that AX linear system plus b. Then, we apply this nonlinear transformation, tanh. But if you wanted to use sigmoid, you could do that. The last layer is slightly different. We're not running tanh on the last layer, we're actually running softmax. This is a classification problem, so we apply softmax to the output of X as opposed to tanh. And that's the output layer.

In the constructor, we've computed the first forward step and our first epoch:

```
    # for each iteration, feed X through the network, compute the loss,
    # and back-propagate the error to correct the weights.
    for _ in xrange(n_iter):
        # compute the product of X on the hidden layers (the output of
        # the network)
        out, layer_results = self._forward_step(X, weights, biases)

        # compute the loss on the output
        loss = _calculate_loss(truth=y, preds=out, weights=weights,
                               l2=self.regularization)
        train_loss.append(loss)

        # now back-propagate to correct the weights and biases via
        # gradient descent
        self._back_propagate(y, out, layer_results, weights,
                             biases, learning_rate,
                             self.regularization)
```

Now we want to calculate the loss; the loss is just that log loss that we saw previously. We're going to track loss per epoch here in train_loss. If you want to speed this up, you might only calculate the loss, say, every five iterations. In the following backpropagation example, we will get a clever idea regarding how we implement these gradients in a fashion that's a bit more extensible than the two-layer example from the last one.

Now, in the backpropagation function, we compute delta again, which is the probabilities of each of the classes minus the truth indices:

```
probas[range(n_samples), truth] -= 1.
# iterate back through the layers computing the deltas (derivatives)
 last_delta = probas
 for next_weights, next_biases, layer_res in \
 zip(weights[::-1], biases[::-1], layer_results[::-1]):
# the gradient for this layer is equivalent to the previous delta
# multiplied by the intermittent layer result
 d_W = layer_res.T.dot(last_delta)
# column sums of the (just-computed) delta is the derivative
# of the biases
 d_b = np.sum(last_delta, axis=0)
# set the next delta for the next iter
 last_delta = last_delta.dot(next_weights.T) * \
 (1. - np.power(layer_res, 2.))
# update the weights gradient with the L2 regularization term
 d_W += l2 * next_weights
# update the weights in this layer. The learning rate governs how
# quickly we descend the gradient
 next_weights += -learning_rate * d_W
 next_biases += -learning_rate * d_b
```

That's our first delta. And now, iteratively, what we're going to do is compute the derivative as that layer's result times the current delta. We start out with the current delta of these probabilities that we just subtracted from. So, now that we've got our gradient, we can compute the derivative of our biases by summing over the columns in the derivative. Now we have the derivative of the biases, and we're going to compute the next delta for the next time we iterate through this. The way we use regularization is by multiplying the regularization by next_weights. So, next_weights is the weight's matrix that we will compute the gradient against. We regularize it and add that to the derivative, and then we are going to adjust the weights. So, we can add learning_rate times the delta, or the gradient, and we do the same for our biases. We've changed next_weights and next_biases inside of weights and biases. This is a void function. It doesn't return anything because it all happened in place.

Now, weights and biases have been iteratively updated. And the next time we progress through the iteration – the next epoch—we should see a lower error. As such, we'll continue this through the number of iterations, progress through all of our epochs, and save our weights and biases. Then, we will produce a prediction and compute those probabilities by doing a forward pass with the softmax at the very end. Take the argmax of the column: that's the class that has the highest probability. And that's what we return in a squashed vector.

In the `example_mlp_classifier` file, we use a similar dataset to what we use in decision tree classification, which are these `multivariate_normal` bubbles that are kind of clusters, in our two-dimensional space. We'll do `train_test_split` as usual:

```
# Fit a simple neural network
n_iter = 4
hidden = (10,)
clf = NeuralNetClassifier(X_train, y_train, hidden=hidden, n_iter=n_iter,
                          learning_rate=0.001, random_state=42)
print("Loss per training iteration: %r" % clf.train_loss)

pred = clf.predict(X_test)
clf_accuracy = accuracy_score(y_test, pred)
print("Test accuracy (hidden=%s): %.3f" % (str(hidden), clf_accuracy))

#
##############################################################################
##
# Fit a more complex neural network
n_iter2 = 150
hidden2 = (25, 25)
clf2 = NeuralNetClassifier(X_train, y_train, hidden=hidden2,
n_iter=n_iter2,
                           learning_rate=0.001, random_state=42)

pred2 = clf2.predict(X_test)
clf_accuracy2 = accuracy_score(y_test, pred2)
print("Test accuracy (hidden=%s): %.3f" % (str(hidden2), clf_accuracy2))
```

And now we're going to train two neural networks. The first one is only going to use four iterations and have a single hidden layer of 10 units. The second one is a little more complex. We're going to do 150 iterations with two hidden layers of 25 units each.

So, we run the `example_mlp_classifier.py` file:

```
(packt-sml) test@test-Veriton-Series:~/Downloads/Hands-on-Supervised-Machine-Learning-with-Python-master/examples/neural_net$ python
example_mlp_classifier.py
Loss per training iteration: [0.7054934135117192, 0.802221719818304, 0.3064944994452768, 0.5678602364503312]
Test accuracy (hidden=(10,)): 0.944
Test accuracy (hidden=(25, 25)): 1.000
```

We got a pretty good test accuracy with a single hidden layer of 10 units: 94.4 percent. But you can see that we almost get 100 percent if we have two hidden layers at 25 each. We also have the training iterations for the first one.

You can see in the following graph how the loss kind of jitters around a bit:

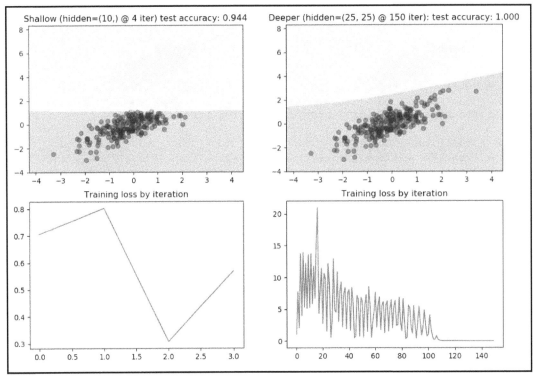

But over time, that loss decreases. It's not guaranteed to be a perfect drop and it might jump up or drop down a bit, but we can see that, over time, our loss hits a point where it's very small. This function that we've learned here in the more complex one is a really interesting nonlinear decision boundary. It has a little bit of trouble classifying these border points, but this is how we can use a neural network to learn a function that's much more complex than something that a logistic regression can learn.

Using transfer learning

In this section, we're going to take it one step further and explore the question of whether a neural network could learn from other neural networks and what they've already learned. We'll start by covering the concept of transfer learning, and then we'll get into some Python code.

Transfer learning is essentially the Frankenstein's monster of machine learning. The idea arose from this question: how can I take what some other network has already learned and go from there? We're basically going to do a brain splice between several different networks. This can be extremely valuable in cases where a network is trained on data that you don't have access to or the training process is the one that would have taken hours or days, as is commonly the case in text or image processing domains.

We don't want to retrain our model because it would take forever, but we want to take what we've already learned about the other two classes and start learning something else about the other class. Rather than retrain the whole thing, we can just use transfer learning to pick up where we left off. So, now that you have the idea and the concept behind it, let's look at how that's going to be applied to the existing multilayer perceptron framework that we're now familiar with.

In the `transfer.py` file, starting with `TransferLearningClassifier`, there's one more argument than there was in `MLPClassifier:` and that's the pretrained network. That can either be `NeuralNetClassifier` or `TransferLearningClassifier`. But we're just going to take `NeuralNetClassifier` for this example. Similar to the MLP constructor, we're going to spend the first few lines saving everything as self attributes, and then we're going to make sure that whatever you've passed in as the pretrained network is going to be some form of `NeuralMixin`:

```
    def __init__(self, X, y, pretrained, hidden=(25,), n_iter=10,
                 regularization=0.01, learning_rate=0.001,
random_state=42):

        # initialize via the NN static method
        self.hidden = hidden
        self.random_state = random_state
        self.n_iter = n_iter
        self.learning_rate = learning_rate
        self.regularization = regularization

        # this is the previous model
        self.model = pretrained

        # assert that it's a neural net or we'll break down later
        assert isinstance(pretrained, NeuralMixin), \
            "Pre-trained model must be a neural network!"

        # initialize weights, biases, etc. for THE TRAINABLE LAYERS ONLY!
        pt_w, pt_b =
pretrained.export_weights_and_biases(output_layer=False)
        X, y, weights, biases = NeuralNetClassifier._init_weights_biases(
            X, y, hidden, random_state,
```

```
                        # use as the last dim the column dimension of the last weights
                        # (the ones BEFORE the output layer, that is)
                        last_dim=pt_w[-1].shape[1])
```

Because we have to have access to the weights and the biases from the previous classes, we get the pretrained weights and the pretrained biases. We only want to initialize the new weights and biases that we can kind of stack on to the end. So, if we have a network of four layers before, those are just going to be ancillary. We're not going to train those—we're just going to freeze them. Then, we want to stack a few layers on the end that we can train and teach new features—new characteristics about the new classes we may want to predict. We're going to do the initialized weights and biases only for the new weights and biases.

Epochs look slightly different; they look a lot like MLPs, but there's a little bit of difference.

So, for each epoch, we're going to perform one pretrained forward step. Basically, all we're going to do here is that for each of those layers in the pretrained weights and biases, we're going to compute $AX + b$ with our `tanh` function on it. Notice that even on the output layer, rather than compute a softmax, we're going to compute `tanh`, because we're not interested in getting those class probabilities anymore. Now we just want to pipe it into the next layer. So, we're going to use whatever that activation function is. It could be `sigmoid` or `relu`.

Now we want to take a forward step on the existing or the new weights and bias layers that we do want to train:

```
            train_loss = []
            for _ in xrange(n_iter):
                # first, pass the input data through the pre-trained model's
                # hidden layers. Do not pass it through the last layer,
however,
                # since we don't want its output from the softmax layer.
                X_transform = _pretrained_forward_step(X, pt_w, pt_b)

                # NOW we complete a forward step on THIS model's
                # untrained weights/biases
                out, layer_results = NeuralNetClassifier._forward_step(
                    X_transform, weights, biases)

                # compute the loss on the output
                loss = _calculate_loss(truth=y, preds=out, weights=pt_w +
weights,
                                        l2=self.regularization)
                train_loss.append(loss)

                # now back-propagate to correct THIS MODEL's weights and biases
via
                # gradient descent. NOTE we do NOT adjust the pre-trained
```

model's
```
        # weights!!!
        NeuralNetClassifier._back_propagate(
            truth=y, probas=out, layer_results=layer_results,
            weights=weights, biases=biases,
            learning_rate=learning_rate,
            l2=self.regularization)
```

We're going to calculate `loss`, and then we're going to backpropagate only on the new layers. So, we're not training the old weights and biases at all, but we are doing that to the new ones.

The predictions are slightly different:

```
    def predict(self, X):
        # compute the probabilities and then get the argmax for each class
        probas = self.predict_proba(X)

        # we want the argmaxes of each row
        return np.argmax(probas, axis=1)

    def predict_proba(self, X):
        # Compute a forward step with the pre-trained model first:
        pt_w, pt_b = \
    self.model.export_weights_and_biases(output_layer=False)
        X_transform = _pretrained_forward_step(X, pt_w, pt_b)

        # and then complete a forward step with the trained weights and
    biases
        return NeuralNetClassifier._forward_step(
            X_transform, self.weights, self.biases)[0]

    def export_weights_and_biases(self, output_layer=True):
        pt_weights, pt_biases = \
            self.model.export_weights_and_biases(output_layer=False)
        w = pt_weights + self.weights
        b = pt_biases + self.biases

        if output_layer:
            return w, b
        return w[:-1], b[:-1]
```

Rather than just compute that single forward step, we're going to compute the pretrained forward step, again, because we don't want that softmax in the end of the other network. Then, we will compute the normal forward step with the output of the pretrained forward step, which will stack the softmax onto the end.

For the predictions, again, we're taking `argmax` of the columns. That is, getting the highest probability class from the predict probabilities.

Let's look at an example file. This is going to look a lot like what we set up in our previous MLP example, except we have two datasets:

```
# these are the majority classes
n_obs = 1250
x1 = rs.multivariate_normal(mean=[0, 0], cov=covariance, size=n_obs)
x2 = rs.multivariate_normal(mean=[1, 5], cov=covariance, size=n_obs)

# this is the minority class
x3 = rs.multivariate_normal(mean=[0.85, 3.25], cov=[[1., .5], [1.25,
0.85]],
                            size=n_obs // 3)

# this is what the FIRST network will be trained on
n_first = int(0.8 * n_obs)
X = np.vstack((x1[:n_first], x2[:n_first])).astype(np.float32)
y = np.hstack((np.zeros(n_first), np.ones(n_first))).astype(int)

# this is what the SECOND network will be trained on
X2 = np.vstack((x1[n_first:], x2[n_first:], x3)).astype(np.float32)
y2 = np.hstack((np.zeros(n_obs - n_first),
                np.ones(n_obs - n_first),
                np.ones(x3.shape[0]) * 2)).astype(int)
```

The first one is going to have those two blobs: the `multivariate_normal` blobs that we've been using and the majority class. The third here is going to stack this third class in between the two. Our transfer learning task is going to be learning this new class based on what it's already learned from the binary classification example.

Let's fit the first neural network that we'll use, which is our pretrained network:

```
# Fit the transfer network - train one more layer with a new class
t_hidden = (15,)
t_iter = 25
transfer = TransferLearningClassifier(X2_train, y2_train, pretrained=clf,
                                      hidden=t_hidden, n_iter=t_iter,
                                      random_state=42)

t_pred = transfer.predict(X2_test)
trans_accuracy = accuracy_score(y2_test, t_pred)
print("Test accuracy (hidden=%s): %.3f" % (str(hidden + t_hidden),
                                           trans_accuracy))
```

This is going to be very similar to what we saw in the first example, where we have a two-layer network with 25 units in each layer. We're going to fit 75 epochs with a pretty low learning rate and we'll see how it does on learning the binary classification task.

Now, let's say we're predicting some type of disease, and there's type one something and type two something. I'm not going to use diabetes because there's only two types. But let's say, a third type comes out. Maybe it's a type of Zika virus, and we want to predict whether this new class is present in a patient who comes in. We don't want to retrain everything, because it's going to take forever, perhaps. So, we're going to just stack this new layer on the end that says learn these new features about this third class. And then we'll produce a new output layer for three classes rather than two. We're only going to do 25 new epochs, just based on what we've already learned from the previous binary classification task. We want to see if we can learn this new class without retraining everything. And that's all we're going to do here:

```
# Fit the transfer network - train one more layer with a new class
t_hidden = (15,)
t_iter = 25
transfer = TransferLearningClassifier(X2_train, y2_train, pretrained=clf,
                                      hidden=t_hidden, n_iter=t_iter,
                                      random_state=42)

t_pred = transfer.predict(X2_test)
trans_accuracy = accuracy_score(y2_test, t_pred)
print("Test accuracy (hidden=%s): %.3f" % (str(hidden + t_hidden),
                                           trans_accuracy))
```

And then we're going to plot both out so you can see the decision boundary from both the binary and this three-class classification problem.

Let's run an example of transfer learning:

```
(packt-sml) test@test-Veriton-Series:~/Downloads/Hands-on-Supervised-Machine-Learning-with-Python-master/examples/neural_net$ python
example_transfer_learning.py
example_transfer_learning.py:27: RuntimeWarning: covariance is not symmetric positive-semidefinite.
  size=n_obs // 3)
Test accuracy (hidden=(25, 25)): 1.000
Test accuracy (hidden=(25, 25, 15)): 0.952
```

Our test accuracy is down to 95.2 percent.

You can see in the following graph that we are able to learn a complex decision boundary in the binary classification task:

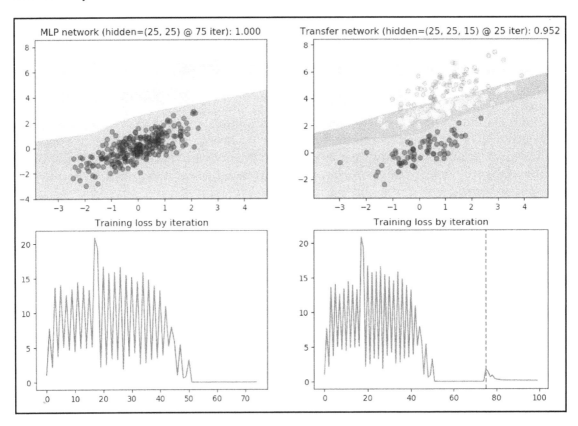

And then we took that and we said let's do transfer learning with a new class, and we were still able to learn it really well. So, now we've learned the second decision boundary that we built on top of our initial decision boundary and it looks really good. So, we get 95.2 percent accuracy.

Summary

Transfer learning is a flexible concept that'll allow you to stack networks together to accomplish far more complex tasks than you thought possible. We covered recommender systems and collaborative filtering in particular, and then we looked at matrix factorization techniques and how to supplement your recommenders with content-based similarities. Lastly, we worked with neural networks and transfer learning.

Other Books You May Enjoy

If you enjoyed this book, you may be interested in these other books by Packt:

Hands-On Unsupervised Learning with Python
Giuseppe Bonaccorso

ISBN: 9781789348279

- Use cluster algorithms to identify and optimize natural groups of data
- Explore advanced non-linear and hierarchical clustering in action
- Soft label assignments for fuzzy c-means and Gaussian mixture models
- Detect anomalies through density estimation
- Perform principal component analysis using neural network models
- Create unsupervised models using GANs

Python Machine Learning By Example - Second Edition
Yuxi (Hayden) Liu

ISBN: 9781789616729

- Understand the important concepts in machine learning and data science
- Use Python to explore the world of data mining and analytics
- Scale up model training using varied data complexities with Apache Spark
- Delve deep into text and NLP using Python libraries such NLTK and gensim
- Select and build an ML model and evaluate and optimize its performance
- Implement ML algorithms from scratch in Python, TensorFlow, and scikit-learn

Leave a review - let other readers know what you think

Please share your thoughts on this book with others by leaving a review on the site that you bought it from. If you purchased the book from Amazon, please leave us an honest review on this book's Amazon page. This is vital so that other potential readers can see and use your unbiased opinion to make purchasing decisions, we can understand what our customers think about our products, and our authors can see your feedback on the title that they have worked with Packt to create. It will only take a few minutes of your time, but is valuable to other potential customers, our authors, and Packt. Thank you!

Index

S

scikit-learn library
  used, for splitting data 30
Spam dataset 6
Sum of Squared Error (SSE) 23
supervised learning in action
  example 10
supervised machine learning
  about 18, 19, 20, 21
  example 6, 7, 8, 9

T

Training score 10, 67

U

transfer learning
  using 138, 139, 141, 142, 143, 144

underfitting 61
unsupervised machine learning 21

V

Validation score 10, 67
variance trade-off
  about 64
  error terms 64
  error, due to 65

www.ingramcontent.com/pod-product-compliance
Lightning Source LLC
Chambersburg PA
CBHW080534060326
40690CB00022B/5121